# STARTING A SINGLE ADULT MINISTRY

## SUE NILSON • ANDY MORGAN

**SiNGLES**
*Ministry Resources*

DAVID C. COOK PUBLISHING CO.
ELGIN, ILLINOIS 60120

SINGLES MINISTRY RESOURCES is a division of Cook Communications Ministries. In fulfilling its mission to encourage the acceptance of Jesus Christ as personal Savior and to contribute to the teaching and putting into practice of His two great commandments, the Foundation creates and disseminates Christian communication materials and services to people throughout the world. SINGLES MINISTRY RESOURCES provides training seminars, a national convention, a journal, and resources materials to assist churches in developing a ministry with single adults that will encourage growth in loving God and each other.

*Starting a Single Adult Ministry*

©1994 by David C. Cook Publishing Company

Published by David C. Cook Publishing Company. All rights reserved. Unless otherwise noted in the text, no part of this publication may be reproduced in any form without written permission from the publishers at 850 North Grove Avenue, Elgin, IL 60120.

Unless otherwise noted, Scripture in this publication is from the Holy Bible: New International Version (NIV), copyright © 1973, 1978, 1984, International Bible Society, used by permission of Zondervan Bible Publishers.

Cover illustration by Burton Morris, represented by Creative Freelancers.

Printed in the United States of America.

# Contents

**12  WHY SINGLES MINISTRIES FAIL AND WHAT TO DO ABOUT IT**            171

It helps to learn ahead of time how to avoid common pitfalls that short-circuit many singles ministries.  Similarly, proven principles that lead to success are crucial to incorporate into your group right from the beginning.

## REPRODUCIBLE RESOURCES

# CHARTS, ETC.

# How to Get the Most Out of This Book

So—you're beginning the quest for a singles ministry at your church! Or you have a singles group already in place, but you're looking for ways to improve the program you have? Welcome to *Starting a Single Adult Ministry* and a multitude of ideas and insights which can help you begin and develop a singles outreach with integrity, quality, and purpose.

This book is not an exhaustive encyclopedia blanketing every last corner of the subject of ministry with single adults. (Refer to the bibliography, page 190, for a list of many other helpful resources.) Rather, it provides tools to help you start your singles ministry journey with some basic "tried and true" principles of program design. It can also help you avoid common setbacks which frequently short-circuit fledgling singles groups. Launching, developing, and evolving a single adult ministry at your church is a *process,* not a destination.

Before beginning to read this book, take a look at the table of contents. Note that the material is arranged to lead you through the process of starting a singles ministry—from evaluating your needs and setting, right through quality programming, recruiting volunteers, publicity, and an appendix called "Tools for the Leader." A chapter called "Especially for Small Churches," is also included because singles ministry in a small church setting presents some unique characteristics you may need to address.

If you are just starting out in singles ministry, begin with Chapter 1 and work your way through the rest of the chapters in order, covering all the bases. If you're looking for specific information, flip to the chapters that interest you.

Cross-references throughout the book will alert you to other places where certain subjects are discussed. If you see an arrow (▶) while reading, look for a matching arrow and related comments in the margin. At the end of every chapter are reproducible resource pages to assist you and your planning team as you build a singles ministry together. These pages are identified with a special icon 📝 and may be reproduced without further written permission from the publisher.

No time in history has been better than the present to become involved in ministry with single adults. The good news is that the last few years have brought a publishing surge of helpful resources and curriculum tailored specifically for use and support in this area of ministry. For example, just before the manuscript for this book was completed, an outstanding research report published by George Barna, *Unmarried America* (Glendale, CA: Barna Research Group, 1993), became available. Use this report and other emerging data (many of which are listed in the Appendix) about single adults in America as you prayerfully prepare and unfold your singles ministry outreach.

May God bless your service for and with single adults! May this book be a bridge into meaningful ministry for you and for those who share your dreams of reaching out to adult singles.

# Thank You

We acknowledge a great indebtedness to all those across the country who have been "pioneers" in the field of single adult ministry, and whose words of wisdom and insight have been quoted throughout the following chapters. In addition, we would like to thank the following individuals who read and critiqued the manuscript, offered valuable insight, and contributed in a variety of ways to the fruition of this project: Linda Ames, Roger Baddeley, Chuck Farah, Jeanette Gardner, Gloria Gustafson, Jerry Jones, Scott Leigh, Cal Marcum, Amy Nilson, Anthony Pappas, and Sharon Schulenberg.

We also thank senior minister Cecil Bliss and the staff at St. Mark's United Methodist Church in Lincoln, Nebraska, whose quest for implementing dynamic church growth principles has dramatically impacted our understanding of how to do singles ministry within the context of the congregation as a whole.

Most importantly, we dedicate this book to all the single adults with whom we have worked throughout our years of ministry. Ultimately, it has been their committed vision that has inspired, equipped, and motivated us to write about the fine art of single adult ministry.

## CHAPTER 1

# Does Your Church Really Need a Singles Ministry?

Single Adult Ministry conferences, seminars, and workshops are increasingly common across the country. Participants are laypersons, staff workers, and ministers. Some are associated with "mega-churches" having thousands of members. Others come from rural communities with congregations of less than fifty people. Though church size and denomination may vary, everyone arrives asking the same basic questions:

• How do we create a single adult ministry that will last?

• How can we get support from the congregation?

• How do we attract new singles to our group?

• How do we keep a singles program going?

• How do we find and sustain leadership for a singles ministry?

Often these questions are from eager "beginners" to single adult ministry. But just as often, these questions come from laypersons or church workers who have struggled with the unique challenges of ministry with single adults. They are uncertain whether or not their labors have produced any fruit.

Rather than trying to sell you on the necessity of having a singles ministry at your church, the goals for *Starting a Single Adult Ministry* are these:

• To provide tools by which you can assess whether or not your church needs a singles ministry *program* (and not every church does—but every church needs to have a ministry with single adults).

• To help answer the "how-to" questions about singles ministry for churches that do need a singles ministry program, and to offer specific, practical suggestions about the best ways to begin and sustain the efforts.

• To suggest additional resources for support in developing a healthy, well-balanced singles ministry program.

*Always remember that ministry with single adults is an art, not a science.* There is no one sure-fire, guaranteed formula for success that works for every church. Consider the information in these pages as simply suggestions and recommendations that must be tailored to your unique church setting.

Terry Hershey, author of *Giving the Ministry Away*, says, "Right ministry is a result of right thinking."[1] It takes prayer, thoughtful evaluation of your own congregation's situation, plus planning, in order to effectively address the specific needs of the single adults in your church and community.

## FEASIBILITY STUDY

This first chapter will help you clarify whether there is a need for a singles ministry program in your church and where to begin. Answering the following six questions will help you develop a foundation for your program that has definition,

---

## Why Do Singles Ministries Fail?

• Because a church feels it "should have a singles ministry," and not because the actual factors support that intention. (As you proceed through this chapter and evaluate whether there is a need in your congregation, remember that not every church needs to have an established singles program—but every church can minister to single adults.)

• Because some churches simply look at what singles programs work in other churches and attempt to copy those programs. (By doing this, however, a congregation misses the goal of intentional, targeted ministry with the single adults of its own membership and surrounding community.)

purpose, and support. *Don't answer these six questions only!* At every stage, include other questions in order to gain as much input as possible. ▶

### 1. Why should you start a single adult ministry in your church?

The most successful ministry programs are based upon the real needs of the participants, the target audience. You can only discover those needs by taking the pulse of your church and community. Who needs the singles ministry—attenders at your church or the community in general? Are any single adults in the church actually asking for a singles ministry? Have numerous people volunteered to help plan and attend future activities, or is this the demand of just one or two?

Many of the single adults in your church may have already found a way to serve, a sense of belonging, and a circle of friends in the congregation. They might not be interested in a program just for singles. Designing your ministry for these single adults who are already integrated into the congregation is not the way to create a successful outreach. Instead, tar-

get your singles program to involve and empower single adults who are not already actively involved in the church. But don't be surprised if (after you have a healthy singles program in place) you're eventually joined by the adult singles who are already serving in the congregation. A strong, vibrant ministry can be very attractive to most single adults.

The interdenominational Willow Creek Community Church, in Barrington, Illinois, is a good example of developing a "need-based" ministry. For years, Willow Creek Church was just an idea in the minds of a small group of hopeful, committed individuals. They canvassed the community in which the church would be located, interviewed hundreds of people about their perceptions, needs, and desires for a church and church-related programs.

After studying the results of this comprehensive research, the congregation was launched. Today more than 15,000 people attend. Why? One reason is that this church responds to the real needs of the people they are trying to reach—the surrounding community—rather than

◀Resource 1, "Does Our Church Really Need a Singles Ministry?" page 19, summarizes the six basic feasibility questions. It may be photocopied and used as a discussion guide by your church, committee, task force, or feasibility study group.

---

## What Are Your Reasons for Starting a Singles Ministry?

Clarify whether or not you have sound reasons for starting a singles ministry at your church. Make sure you're not starting a singles ministry for the wrong reasons. Compare your situation with the following list.

*Reasons to start a singles ministry in your church:*

• Develop a more effective outreach to the growing number of single adults in your church and community.

• Enhance overall church growth.

• Help fulfill Christ's "Great Commission" by sharing the Gospel with every segment of your community.

• Help renew the vision and purpose of your congregation.

• Meet the unique needs of single adults who want spiritual growth, healing opportunities, and social fellowship.

*Reasons not to start a singles ministry in your church:*

• Just to give a few single adults "something to be in charge of" or "something to do."

• Because other churches in your area have a singles program.

• Because some of the single adults in your church are looking for a mate.

• Because it has been mandated (decreed, ordered) by the senior pastor or demanded by a few outspoken single adults who want someone else to start it for them.

forming their own assumptions about what prospective attenders want.

Developing a specialized program like a singles ministry is no different. The events and activities—the entire ministry to singles—must respond to the needs of the target group of singles the church hopes to reach. "Intentional ministry" is the key.

---

*"Research indicates that people experiencing transition and tension are open to the Spirit of Christ and to making new commitments. Clearly, this presents the church with an exciting opportunity for ministry and evangelism. A singles program in the local church that seeks to minister to those who are hurting and in need of loving care—provided in the context of commitment to Jesus Christ as Lord and Savior—communicates the Gospel."* —ROBERT PIERSON, SENIOR MINISTER AT CHRIST UNITED METHODIST CHURCH, TULSA, OKLAHOMA[2]

---

### 2. Does a significant single adult population already attend your church or live in the neighborhood or community?

To decide if a singles ministry is feasible in your church, find out how many adult singles already attend your church—on Sunday mornings and throughout the week at other activities. Your church may have accurate files to produce this data conveniently. Or, you may need to ask the senior minister to pass out a simple survey on one or two Sundays during morning services to find out how many singles are present and to learn more about their life profiles. ◄

From the church files or the survey data, discern the age groups of the singles attending your church (or living in your community). Are they mostly young adults? Single parents with children? Retirement-aged widows? Do any of these categories show predominant life-styles such as white collar, blue collar, students,

► For information about Single Adults (Demographics and Stats), see Resource 4, "Special 'State of the Singles' Report," pages 23 and 24.

► For tools to help you collect information about single adults in your church and community, see Resources 2 and 3, pages 21 and 22.

unemployed? This information is essential for tailoring your program to the needs and interests of those you want to reach. ◄

One mistake that some churchworkers make is to assume just the opposite: that all single persons enjoy, and benefit from, the same types of programs. At a national church growth conference, one frustrated Christian education director said her church had "tried" singles ministry, but had failed.

"We had three potluck dinners, but only two people attended each," she explained sadly. When asked what type of singles attended her church, she described a large group of young adults.

"Maybe young adults don't like potluck dinners?" someone suggested. The Christian education director looked bewildered.

"Well," she reflected, "the pastor and I decided to plan potluck dinners for them. Why, everyone knows single people should like potluck dinners since they don't have families to go home to!"

This church staff operated upon general assumptions they had made about single persons, rather than talking to single adults about their life-styles and creating strategies to target their interests and needs. The Christian education director and pastor wanted to minister to the singles, rather than ministering with them and equipping them to have their own ministry.

Beyond the congregational survey data, a broader look at this question should also include facts about the church's neighborhood or surrounding community. Does the area house a significant single adult population? Is your church near apartment complexes or condominiums? Are the homes filled with young adults, families, or retired older adults? Is your church near a shopping center or stores frequented by single adults? Are schools or a day care center nearby? Does your neighborhood contain a health club? All of these factors signal a potential source of prospects for your singles events, and will help you target need-based programs and activities for singles.

Take intentional stock of your neighborhood and community to glean this information. If you don't like researching, find someone who does. Researching—becoming knowledgable about the audience you are trying to reach—is necessary for success.

### 3. What are the pastoral and congregational attitudes about single adult ministry?

In many ways, this question is one of the most crucial. Have you thoroughly talked with the senior pastor or the staff of your congregation? To what degree do these people support the prospect of a singles ministry at your church?

Singles ministries that are supported from the pulpit and integrated into the church's structure usually have the best chance to take root and grow. "Lip service" by the church's administration is inadequate. For a singles program to thrive, both the pastor and the staff must support it with a comprehensive attitude of inclusiveness toward singles and enthusiasm about a singles ministry.

The pastor and staff must set an example for the congregation with their words, by displaying sensitivity in all-church programming—even by naming various church activities. For example, if it's intended to be an all-church "Valentine Couples Dinner," it might be renamed "Valentine's Day Dinner" to include those without spouses or dates.

*What is your senior pastor's attitude toward singles?* Ward Presbyterian Church in Livonia, Michigan, annually reaches 3,500 persons through its single adult ministry. One reason why a handful of singles meeting in a garage grew into this enormous outreach is because the senior pastor supported the singles ministry venture from the beginning by providing:

• Emphasis and information about singles ministry from the pulpit.

• Budget support.

• Involvement of the boards and elders in the vision to reach single adults.

• Singles ministry office space.

• Adequate singles ministry staff.

When the Ward single adults perceived they were welcomed, accepted, and affirmed they became increasingly committed to the ministry programs. But without that support, would Ward's "Singlepoint Ministry" ever have grown as it has? Doubtful. The senior pastor's support certainly made a difference in this church—and it will in yours, too.

*What is your congregation's general attitude about singleness?* No matter how much a congregation theoretically supports single adults, the singles who attend your church must feel that support or they will "vote with their feet" and leave.

"We have a singles Sunday class," a single adult in one large southern church reported. "But we had to move its loca-

---

## Single Adult Population Data

Where can you find data about the single adult population in your neighborhood, city, or region? Your state's Department of Economic Development can provide current demographic data. Or, the U.S. Census Bureau's new national "State Data Center Program," has offices in all fifty states geared to supply local and regional demographic information. For the address and phone number of the "State Data Center" nearest you, call the Washington D.C. Data Center Program headquarters at 301/763-1580. ▶

◀ For collecting data, see Resource 4, page 23.

tion. The class met next door to the young marrieds' class, and they didn't like having the singles class so close. We were all walking in and out of our classrooms at the same time." No wonder this singles ministry was struggling! Though the theology of this church's denomination included singles, the marrieds in the congregation obviously felt threatened by them.

While the initial congregational attitude is important, don't view it as the absolute barometer of your ministry's success. As the church leaders continually "educate" the congregation about including single adults, an indifferent or negative attitude can and will change. Time, patience, and commitment are necessary. ◄

► Are you looking for ways to change your church's attitude about single adults and create a good image for and within your future singles ministry? See Chapter 2.

*Is ministry with single persons (including the divorced) compatible with your church's theology?* Have you checked the doctrinal statements from your church to see if they mention specific doctrinal positions about singleness and divorce? If so, are those statements and your intentions for single adult ministry compatible?

Churches with strict guidelines about divorce and remarriage often struggle to establish a ministry with divorced persons, but do well with never-married and widowed adults. Again, this is important to consider when deciding if your church should have a singles ministry—and, if so, what "target groups" of single adults you will try to reach. Single adults consid-

ering involvement in your church will want to know the church's stance on both divorce and remarriage. Know the answers and have that information available.

*Is ministry with single people compatible with the purpose statement or mission statement of your church?* Many churches have a general (or specific) mission or purpose statement to help the church committees and planning boards stay on track with total church ministry. If your church has such a statement, does it include singles ministry? If not, you may consider working with your church's governing board to add a clause about specific ministry with single adults. As a result, all the parts of the church structure will have singles ministry as part of their general purpose.

**4. Could this new ministry find financial support in the church budget or from other sources?**

In order to begin even a very basic ministry with singles, you must have an idea for the financial underwriting for your program. Can the church budget cover any of your singles activities? If not, how will you pay for Sunday school materials, any necessary child care for activities, photocopying for publicity purposes, and other expenses? Will the congregation take a special offering on a quarterly basis? Will the singles themselves financially support, or help support, this ministry? Chapter 9 provides more informa-

---

## How Open Is Your Church to Single Adults?

How do single adults visiting your church perceive its atmosphere? According to the study *Single Adults in America*, by George Barna, single adults have definite ideas about what is important to find in a congregation. Ninety-one percent of singles surveyed indicated "making visitors feel welcome" was the most critical element to find in a church. And 70% of those surveyed placed "investing time and effort in close friendships" as their top priority in life. Your church's openness in welcoming adult singles will be pivotal in whether or not you successfully sustain a singles ministry through which friendships between participants can form.[3] How does your congregation rate?

tion about financing your singles ministry.

Whatever the strategy, you must examine your possibilities within the church budget, or at least have realistic and informed ideas about financial resources.

---

*"Suppose one of you wants to build a tower. Will he not first sit down and estimate the cost to see if he has enough money to complete it?"*

—JESUS (LUKE 14:28)

---

### 5. What resources in your church and community are available to help you with single adult programs?

Counselors, teachers, and instructors in your area (from both Christian and secular organizations) may be willing to present programs to your group at little or no cost. Some of these individuals might even be members of your congregation.

Christian counseling centers are excellent resources for speakers and programs. Contact the director of any such center in your area and check on topics, honorariums, and schedule availability.

Perhaps a "speaker's bureau" at the local or regional junior college or university provides inexpensive speakers for groups. Sometimes large medical centers also have speakers who offer programs to groups in the community. Or could a "singles-sensitive" pastor from another congregation lead a seminar or workshop for your group?

Are other single adult ministries already active in your city? Your group could join with one or more of them to hold special single adult activities or retreats. Check the possibilities for these and other already-existing resources which could enhance your group's ministry.

### 6. What will be your working definition of "singles ministry"?

The answer to this question can be short, but must be strategic. Every singles ministry needs a working definition so you will have basic criteria by which to measure whether you are accomplishing your purpose. Without a definition of singles ministry, your only standards will be factors such as how many attended (the "numbers" game) or whether your program was as "good" as another church's (the "comparison" game). As a result, you will never feel you have "arrived" or realize how God is at work among you.

For example, suppose your singles ministry definition is "single adults supporting, caring, and growing together as Christians." According to this definition, five single adults sharing Bible study and snacks meets your goal as well as five hundred attending.

Part of being a singles ministry worker is celebrating the way God is at work with people and between people, never failing to recognize that even two or three individuals meeting together for support and spiritual growth can be a viable ministry. The criteria for defining singles ministry at your church should fit your congregation, your vision, and the singles' needs in

---

## How Big Does Your Group Need to Be?

Singles ministry can occur among a few individuals who meet together for support, prayer, and godly encouragement. Yet at the same time, a singles group that is growing in numbers represents a more exciting entry point for new singles coming into your church. The size of your singles group or program should evolve to be an honest reflection of your church size, or the percentage of singles in your congregation. If it doesn't, you may need to reevaluate. See Chapter 12, "Why Single Ministries Fail and What to Do about It," for more information.

## Singles Ministry or Singles Club?

**How does a singles ministry differ from a singles club?** According to John Bodin, singles minister at Willow Creek, "a singles club is perceived as a place that will meet the social needs of singles. A singles ministry examines the needs of the whole individual." Every singles ministry should consider addressing these four major needs of single adults:
• The need to grow spiritually.
• The need to form healthy relationships and friendships.
• The need for emotional health or healing.
• The need for opportunity to serve others.

your church and community.

Always remember your programs for singles will have the greatest impact and effectiveness when you have thoughtfully prayed, planned, prepared, and laid the groundwork for God to work.

Have you processed all six questions in this chapter? On the following pages you will find reproducible discussion guides, information sheets, and a sample congregational survey. Use these tools to help you and the others working with you discuss the factors in your church's situation where single adults are concerned.

If you find that a viable need exists for a singles ministry at your church, take a look at Chapter 2. As you get started with your group, you'll find help on how to get your head and heart into "singles territory" and how to develop a healthy attitude toward single adults, their needs, and their gifts.

## TOOLS TO HELP YOU

The resource sheets on the following pages will help you collect information regarding single adults in your church and community and determine whether or not your church should establish a single adult ministry.
• **Resource 1, "Does Our Church Really Need a Singles Ministry?"** *(Worksheet)* Use this worksheet to stimulate discussion with others in your church.
• **Resource 2, "Congregational Profile"** *(Worship Service Survey Form)* Have the pastor use this survey to collect useful profile data from all adults (not just singles) who attend the morning worship service. From these forms, draw a profile of the singles who attend your church and collect names and phone numbers of people who are interested in a singles ministry. This will help you later in forming a "dream team" (see Chapter 3).
• **Resource 3, "Single Adult Profile—A Look at Your Neighborhood, City, and Region** *(Data Collection Form)* Use this form to collect data regarding the single adult population in the geographical area surrounding your church.
• **Resource 4, "Special 'State of the Singles' Report"** *(Demographics/Statistics)* Share copies of this report with others in your church to emphasize the potential ministry your church can have with single adults.

# DOES OUR CHURCH REALLY NEED A SINGLES MINISTRY?

Use this page to jot notes, compile general data, and stimulate discussion with others in your church. Data for questions 2 through 6 may be compiled from a congregational survey (see Resource 2) or from existing information about those who attend your church.

**1. Why should we start a single adult ministry in our church?** *(List several reasons.)*

**2. Does a significant single adult population already attend our church or live in the community?** *(Use Resource 3 to collect data about single adults in your community.)*
- Approximately how many single adults already attend our church?_____
- How many are members of our congregation?_____
- How many are ages 20-30? _____ 31-40? _____ 41-50? _____ 51-60? _____ 61 plus?_____
- How many are men?_____ women?_____
- How many are parents with children still at home? _____
- How many are divorced?_____ always single?_____ widowed? _____ separated?_____

**3. What are the pastoral and congregational attitudes toward single adult ministry?**
- Senior pastor's attitude:

- Congregation's general attitude:

*(continued)*

**4. Is ministry with single persons (including the divorced) compatible with our church's theology?** *(Explain.)*

**5. Is ministry with single people compatible with the purpose statement of our church?** *(Obtain and study a copy of the denomination's or church's policy on divorce and remarriage.)*

**6. How will we financially support this ministry?**

**7. What resources in our church and community are available to help us with single adult programs?**

**8. What will be our working definition of "singles ministry"?**

# CONGREGATIONAL PROFILE
## WORSHIP SERVICE SURVEY FORM

Our church is surveying all adults of our congregation (ages 18 and older). Would you please help us by taking a moment to complete the following questions?

**1. Are you a member of this church?** ❏ Yes ❏ No

**2. What is your gender?** ❏ Male ❏ Female

**3. How long have you been attending our church?** _____

**4. How often do you attend our church?** ❏ Regularly (at least once a week) ❏ Frequently (at least twice a month) ❏ Occasionally (at least four to six times a year)

**5. How long does it take to drive from your home to our church?**
❏ Less than ten minutes ❏ 10–15 minutes ❏ 20 minutes or more

**6. Are you involved in leading one of our church's classes, committees, or other volunteer positions?** ❏ Yes ❏ No

**7. What is your age group?** ❏ 20-29 ❏ 30-39 ❏ 40-49 ❏ 50-59 ❏ 60 plus

**8. Do you work outside the home?** ❏ Yes ❏ No

**9. Are you retired?** ❏ Yes ❏ No

**10. If you work outside the home, what do you do?**

**11. Are you a student?** ❏ Yes ❏ No **If yes:** ❏ Full-time ❏ Part-time

**12. Please indicate your current status:**
❏ Married ❏ Always single ❏ Divorced ❏ Separated ❏ Widowed

**13. Do you have children?** ❏ Yes ❏ No **Ages of children**_____

**14. If divorced/separated, do your children live in your home most of the time?** ❏ Yes ❏ No

**15. What could our church do to help you experience a fuller life? Please list any suggestions for special classes, activities, or programs:**

**16. Would you like more information about new church programs that may be of interest to you?** If so, please leave us your name and phone number.

Name_____ Phone _____

# SINGLE ADULT PROFILE—
# A LOOK AT YOUR NEIGHBORHOOD,
# COMMUNITY, CITY, AND REGION

You can get the information for this form from your state's Department of Economic Development (call your state capitol for the phone number). For more detailed information, try the national "State Data Center Program" office in your state, which provides demographic information gathered during the most recent national census. To find the "State Data Center" nearest you, call the Washington D.C. headquarters at 301/763-1580.

**What is the adult (18+) population of our city?**_____

**What percentage of this population is male?**\_\_\_\_\_% **female?**\_\_\_\_\_%

**What percentage of the homes are headed by single parents?** \_\_\_\_\_%

**What is the demographic makeup of our church's neighborhood?** *(Fill in the chart below, showing percentages in each category.)*

| Demographic Makeup of Our Church's Neighborhood | | | | | | |
|---|---|---|---|---|---|---|
| | **TOTAL AGES 20 plus** | **AGES 20-29** | **AGES 30-39** | **AGES 40-49** | **AGES 50-59** | **AGES 60 plus** |
| Never-married men | | | | | | |
| Never-married women | | | | | | |
| Married men | | | | | | |
| Married women | | | | | | |
| Divorced men | | | | | | |
| Divorced women | | | | | | |
| Widowed men | | | | | | |
| Widowed women | | | | | | |
| Single parents (men) | | | | | | |
|   Custodial | | | | | | |
|   Non-custodial | | | | | | |
| Single parents (women) | | | | | | |
|   Custodial | | | | | | |
|   Non-custodial | | | | | | |
| Separated men | | | | | | |
| Separated women | | | | | | |

**Notes about other data that is relevant to our unique situation:**

# SPECIAL "STATE OF THE SINGLES" REPORT

*This "State of the Singles" Report is intended to provide you with a quick snapshot view of some of the statistics, trends, and changes in the single adult population.*

*Use this as a helpful reference (and a possible reminder of one of the reasons God may have positioned you in a ministry with single adults).*

*This can also be an excellent resource tool to help reeducate your senior pastor and other church leaders about the increasing need for ministry with single adults in your church and community.*

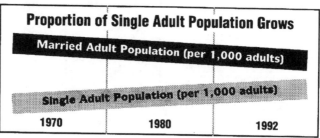

**Proportion of Single Adult Population Grows**

Married Adult Population (per 1,000 adults)

Single Adult Population (per 1,000 adults)

| 1970 | 1980 | 1992 |

 *During the past two decades, the unmarried adult population has grown much more rapidly than the married adult population. That trend continues, according to the most recent U.S. Census Bureau data.*

## Single Adults Continue to Increase as a Percentage of the Total Adult Population

The number of currently married persons has grown 19 percent since 1970 (from 95 million in 1970 to 113 million in 1992), but the proportion they represented of all adults declined from 72 to 61 percent.

The number of unmarried adults* nearly doubled since 1970 (from 38 million to 72 million), and the proportion they represented of all adults rose from 28 to about 40 percent.

Two of the major factors contributing to this change are delayed marriage and increased divorce.

*\*The category "unmarried" includes currently never-married, widowed, and divorced adults.*

## How Many Single Adults* Are There?

As of 1992 (most recent statistics available) there were 72 million single adults, almost 40 percent of the total adult population.*

Here's a quick rundown on the numbers since 1970:

- In 1970 there were 37.5 million single adults
- In 1980, 56.8 million
- In 1990, 69.2 million
- In 1992, 72 million

*\*Ages 18 and up.*

 *Although the divorce rate (as presented by the National Center for Health Statistics) has declined slightly during the early 90s, the divorce ratio is rising. This is because the total number of currently divorced persons has continued to increase more rapidly than the total number of currently married persons.*

## The Divorced Population

Although the never-marrieds make up the largest share of the single adult population, the largest proportional increase of any marital status category has been among divorced persons. Between 1970 and 1992, the number of currently divorced persons quadrupled from 4.3 million to 16.3 million.

The ratio of divorced persons to persons in intact marriages is an index for measuring the increase in divorce. Over the past two decades the ratio has risen from 47 divorced persons per 1,000 persons in intact marriages in 1970 to 152 per 1,000 in 1992.

 *In 1992 more than one quarter of all children in the U.S. (17.5 million) lived with only one parent—double the percentage of 1970 and almost triple that of 1960.*

## Single-Parent Families

Between 1970 and 1992, the proportion of children living with two parents declined from 85 percent to 71 percent, while the proportion living with

*(continued)*

one parent more than doubled from 12 percent to 27 percent.

Children in one-parent situations most often lived with their mother (88 percent in 1992), although the proportion who lived with their father has grown, from 9 percent in 1970 to 12 percent in 1992. Children of divorce make up the largest share of children living with one parent (37 percent), followed by children born to a parent who had never married (34 percent).

 *Never-married persons make up the largest share of single adults (58 percent) and a sizable portion of the total adult population (23 percent). Between 1970 and 1992, the number of never-married adults nearly doubled, from 21 to 42 million.*

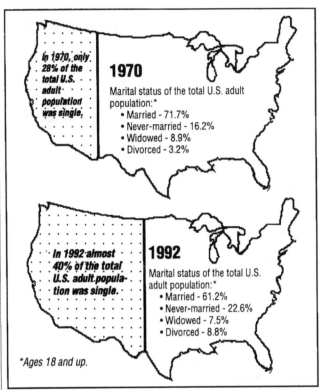

1970
Marital status of the total U.S. adult population:*
• Married - 71.7%
• Never-married - 16.2%
• Widowed - 8.9%
• Divorced - 3.2%

In 1970, only 28% of the total U.S. adult population was single.

1992
Marital status of the total U.S. adult population:*
• Married - 61.2%
• Never-married - 22.6%
• Widowed - 7.5%
• Divorced - 8.8%

In 1992 almost 40% of the total U.S. adult population was single.

*Ages 18 and up.

## Never-Married Single Adults

Since the mid-1950s, when the median age at first marriage was at an all-time low, adults have been waiting longer and longer to marry. The proportions of men and women in their twenties and thirties who have never married have grown substantially since 1970. Among women age 20 to 24, two-thirds had never married in 1992, compared to just over one-third in 1970. Among women in their late twenties and early thirties, the proportions never married tripled between 1970 and 1992 (from 11 to 33 percent for age 25 to 29 and from 6 to 19 percent for age 30 to 34). The proportion for women age 35 to 39 more than doubled, from 5 to 13 percent.

Young men have higher proportions never married than women, as men tend to marry at older ages. In 1992, 80 percent of men age 20 to 24 had never married and nearly 50 percent of men age 25 to 29 had never married (up from 55 and 19 percent respectively).

Among men in their thirties, the proportion never married tripled during the 1970 to 1992 period for age 30 to 34 and more than doubled for age 35 to 39 (from 9 to 29 percent and from 7 to 18 percent respectively).

 *In 1970, there was only one unmarried couple per 100 married couples. By 1992, this ratio had increased to six per 100.*

## Unmarried Couples

In 1992, there were 3.3 million unmarried-couple households, double the number in 1980. The number of unmarried-

couple households is relatively small when compared with the total number of married couples; however, the ratio of unmarried to married couples is growing. In 1970, there was only 1 unmarried couple per 100 married couples. By 1992, this ratio had increased to 6 per 100.

The majority (57 percent) of partners in unmarried-couple households had never been married, 33 percent were divorced, 6 percent were married but not living with their spouse, and 4 percent were widowed.

*(NOTE: An unmarried-couple household, as defined by the Census Bureau, contains only two adults with or without children under 15 years old present in the home. The adults must be of opposite sex and not related to one another.)*

**SOURCES:** *Marital Status and Living Arrangements: March 1992* (Bureau of the Census, U.S. Dept. of Commerce); *New Realities of the American Family* by Ahlburg and DeVita (Population Reference Bureau, August 1992). This report was originally published in *Single Adult Ministries Journal*, Issue #101, '94.

# A Check-Up on Attitudes toward Single Adults

REPRODUCIBLE RESOURCES AT THE END OF THIS CHAPTER

How we think about singleness directly affects the kind of ministry we will have, who will attend, and what will result.

At a regional training event for people involved in single adult ministry, a man said, "I'm only here because our pastor said our church needs a singles group. He asked me to organize it because nobody else would."

By all indications, this individual did not possess deep enthusiasm or a sense of mission and vision for the ministry. And unless his attitude changes, his ministry will probably sputter and die relatively soon.

Your attitude about what you are doing for singles and why you are doing it ultimately dictates the direction and health of your ministry. Your attitude about working with adult singles will also affect the image others will have of the ministry.

If you are a pastor, staff person, or layperson who directs singles work just because "nobody else would do it," your single adults will probably receive a negative message about the value of the program. You may project the image that you are working with a group of needy people out of pity or obligation. This will not help you gain support among the singles themselves or the congregation in general.

---

*[Church] leadership feels caught in a real bind. On one hand, they feel they ought to do something to help address and meet single adult needs. But on the other hand, they feel threatened. They don't know what to do with single adults. Some, it seems, even wish the issue didn't exist.* —LARRY CRABB, FOUNDER OF THE INSTITUTE OF BIBLICAL COUNSELING, DENVER, COLORADO[1]

---

The important key is to develop and nurture your own commitment, vision, and interest in the program you plan to help create and in the singles you wish to reach. Without these ingredients, a single adult ministry—or any ministry you forge in God's name—will never be truly effective or genuine. If established without a good understanding of the target audience, ministries with singles tend to unfold as patronizing programs designed to help hapless individuals who are unfortunate enough to "still be single" and as "holding tanks" for them until they get married (or remarried)!

## TEST YOURSELF![2]
### What Do You Know about Single Adults?
### What Do You Know about the Single Adult Population in General?

Before reading the rest of this chapter, stop a minute to check your knowledge about single adults in America. Take the following test, then check your answers against the answer key, page 28.

**1.** Demographic trends show that by the year 2000, ___ of all adults will be unmarried. **(a)** 25% **(b)** 35% **(c)** 50%

**2.** ___ of all children today are living in a home headed by a single adult.
**(a)** 10% **(b)** 20% **(c)** 30%

**3.** Approximately ___ of all children born in America today are expected to spend some part of their childhood in a single-parent home. **(a)** 10% **(b)** 30% **(c)** 45% **(d)** 60%

**4.** Over the last thirty years, the greatest growth rate in "Unmarried America" has been in ___ adults. In fact, this category makes up six-tenths of "Unmarried America." **(a)** never-married **(b)** divorced **(c)** widowed

**5.** Between 1970 and 1990, the marriage rate in America (the number of marriages per 1,000 adults) fell almost ___. **(a)** 20% **(b)** 30% **(c)** 40% **(d)** 50%

**6.** During this same period (1970–1990), the divorce rate in America (the number of divorces per 1,000 adults) increased by almost ___. **(a)** 10% **(b)** 20% **(c)** 30% **(d)** 40%

**7.** ___ of unchurched adults in America are single. **(a)** 26% **(b)** 37% **(c)** 45% **(d)** 51%

**8.** The least-churched segment of the single adult population of our country are the ___. **(a)** never-married **(b)** divorced **(c)** widowed

**9.** ___ adults tend to be more religious than average, but they tend to see Christianity, not a local church, as relevant to their lives. **(a)** never-married **(b)** divorced **(c)** widowed

**10.** Almost ___ of the births in 1985 were to unmarried women. **(a)** 1 in 4 **(b)** 1 in 12 **(c)** 1 in 16

**11.** Six in ten hopeful never-marrieds listed ___ as one of the most appealing reasons to get married. **(a)** companionship **(b)** having children **(c)** sex

**12.** Today, ___ of all never-marrieds think it wise to cohabit with one's partner before getting married. **(a)** 25% **(b)** 40% **(c)** 60%

**13.** The single adult population's least-favorite method of contact from a church is ___. **(a)** unsolicited mail **(b)** home visit by the pastor **(c)** phone call

**14.** Three-fourths of all ___ adults believe there is no such thing as absolute truth. **(a)** never-married **(b)** divorced **(c)** widowed

**15.** Divorced men are ___ than divorced women to remarry. **(a)** less likely **(b)** more likely

**16.** ___ of all marriages today are remarriages for one or both partners. **(a)** 27% **(b)** 41% **(c)** 46% **(d)** 53%

**17.** Sixty-two percent of all divorced persons feel single-parent homes are ___ compared to any other type of family. **(a)** disadvantaged **(b)** dysfunctional **(c)** no different

**18.** Approximately two-thirds of all divorced people ___ that remarriage for single parents would help everyone in the household be better off. **(a)** believe **(b)** do not believe

**19.** ___ adults are more likely to describe themselves as politically conservative and traditional than are people in other marital categories, including marrieds. **(a)** never-married **(b)** divorced **(c)** widowed

**20.** The only group of single adults who consider money to be especially important in their priorities are the ___. **(a)** never-married **(b)** divorced **(c)** widowed

**21.** The ___ are the most likely group of single adults to believe that in times of trouble, they have no one to turn to for comfort and support. **(a)** never-married **(b)** divorced **(c)** widowed

**22.** The church's loudest cheerleaders are often the ___, half of whom believe Christianity enjoys more influence on Americans today than it did five years ago. **(a)** never-married **(b)** divorced **(c)** widowed

**23.** If current trends continue, ___ of all Americans will be a member of a stepfamily by the year 2000. **(a)** 12% **(b)** 36% **(c)** 50% **(d)** 61%

## EXACTLY WHO ARE SINGLE ADULTS?

Basing your involvement with singles on a positive attitude toward them will infuse what you do with meaning, purpose, and value. Demographic trends show that the percentage of single adults in America is growing. If the current growth trend continues, it is estimated that half of all adults in our country will be single by the turn of the century. ◄

► See chart on page 29.

Let's begin your "attitude inventory" with background information about, and descriptions of, those included in the single adult segment of the population. Single adults fall into three basic categories: (1) the never-married, (2) the divorced, and (3) the widowed. If you plan to work with singles, you must become familiar with the profile of each. You may not target all of these groups and their subgroups for programming in your own singles outreach—but you need to be aware of, and sensitive to, them. ◄

► See page 35 for a quick overview of the various types of single adults, the issues they face, and what the church can offer each.

The following brief descriptions of the three singles categories do not comprehensively cover all the complex issues (and subgroups) involved in each type of singleness, but they can help you discover and clarify your own attitudes about, and understanding of, single adults.

### 1. Never-marrieds

*Description.* Some who have never been married prefer to be called "always-single"; others describe themselves as "never-married." According to the U. S. Census Bureau, of the nearly 36 million people (ages 20+) in this category, over one-third (37 percent) are ages 20 to 24. An additional 38 percent are ages 25 to 34.[3]

*The combination of demographic changes, postponed weddings and forgone marriages rapidly increased the size of never-married America in the last two decades, from 16% of the adult population in 1970 to 23% in 1991. One man in four has never been married, compared to one woman in five. Today 21% of white adults are never-married, compared with 37% of black adults.*

—GEORGE BARNA[4]

Some congregations assume "never-married" is synonymous with the "red convertible myth": that all singles in this category drive red sports cars, party all weekend, and live a footloose and self-indulgent lifestyle. Television and movie portrayals have romanticized and reinforced this stereotype.

But, as with all categories of singleness, never-marrieds represent a broad landscape of diversity. For example, contrary to many people's assumptions, the never-marrieds are not all young adults. In fact, *nearly 40 percent of this group (ages 20+) are over 30 years of age*, and the average age of never-marrieds is on the rise.

Of those who are under 30, over half live with their parents.[5] This reflects the economic times and the fact that it has become increasingly difficult to find jobs and make ends meet.

Some never-marrieds command salaries far above the middle range of earning power; an equal number live below poverty level. Although never-marrieds are predominately college-

---

## Test Yourself Answer Key

**How did you do on the test? Check your answers against the following key.**

| | | | | | |
|---|---|---|---|---|---|
| 1 (c) | 5 (b) | 9 (b) | 13 (b) | 17 (c) | 21 (c) |
| 2 (c) | 6 (d) | 10 (a) | 14 (b) | 18 (b) | 22 (c) |
| 3 (d) | 7 (d) | 11 (b) | 15 (b) | 19 (c) | 23 (c) |
| 4 (a) | 8 (a) | 12 (c) | 16 (c) | 20 (a) | |

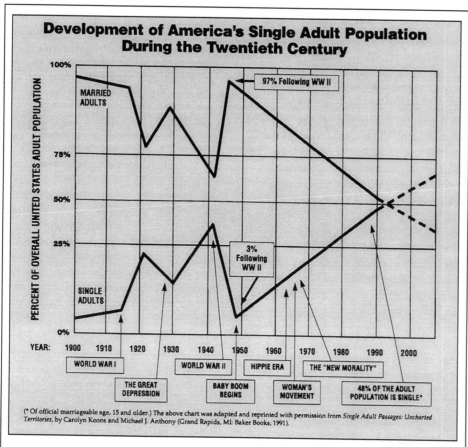

**Development of America's Single Adult Population During the Twentieth Century**

97% Following WW II

MARRIED ADULTS

3% Following WW II

SINGLE ADULTS

PERCENT OF OVERALL UNITED STATES ADULT POPULATION

100%

75%

50%

25%

0%

YEAR: 1900 1910 1920 1930 1940 1950 1960 1970 1980 1990 2000

WORLD WAR I

WORLD WAR II

HIPPIE ERA

THE "NEW MORALITY"

THE GREAT DEPRESSION

BABY BOOM BEGINS

WOMAN'S MOVEMENT

48% OF THE ADULT POPULATION IS SINGLE*

(* Of official marriageable age, 15 and older.) The above chart was adapted and reprinted with permission from *Single Adult Passages: Uncharted Territories*, by Carolyn Koons and Michael J. Anthony (Grand Rapids, MI: Baker Books, 1991).

educated, the overall picture includes many who represent the economically and educationally oppressed. Barna reports that the never-marrieds are the least churched segment of the single adult population in America.[6]

*Key Issues.* What are some central issues for never-marrieds today?

• *Changing sexual values.* According to the 1992 *Family in America Survey,* nearly 80 percent of the never-marrieds who were polled said they already had been involved in a sexual relationship.[7] Secular society no longer demands marriage as the only appropriate realm for sexual activity.

• *Career, income, and possessions.* Never-marrieds place most of their energy in these pursuits, having the freedom to be more centered on personal goals and objectives. Personal happiness and self-fulfillment are high priorities.

• *The death of a dream (and the accompanying grief).* For many never-marrieds over 30 or 35, the issues of dealing with the prospect of never having a mate or children can be a painful pill to swallow. For them, life is not turning out the way they had always expected it to— the way it had for their parents and grandparents. This can be a traumatic time of soul-searching and evaluation.

• *Close friendships.* In recent research by Barna, never-married adults overwhelmingly named "personal friendships" as most desirable of all life attributes, even more than having a close relationship with God or holding a high-paying job.[8]

These key issues offer a general portrait of contemporary never-married single adulthood. However, these issues sometimes exist in the midst of unsettledness and sense of transition, especially for those under age thirty.

Young never-married adults who are "twentysomething" often say they are not "single"—they are just not married yet. Many young adults put off major events like buying a house, trading in a car, investing in furniture, or developing a long-term financial investment plan because they were waiting for marriage before making such "life decisions."

Some never-marrieds find it hard to go ahead with making life decisions alone. Never-married adults who are older than thirty-five frequently complain about feeling "misunderstood" by their married peers, and particularly about feeling left out of the mainstream of the church with its traditional family-oriented activities. They even sometimes feel left out of a singles ministry if it has a heavy emphasis on divorce recovery and single-parent families. Where do they fit?

---

*According to the 1990 U.S. census, 23 million Americans live by themselves. This is a 91% jump for women since 1970, and a 156% increase for men over the same time period. Middle-aged singles are among the fastest-growing of these groups.* [9]

---

**What the church can offer.** Ideally, the church offers never-marrieds a place to develop a sense of belonging within the church family and a place to form healthy adult relationships. A singles ministry can create the kind of accepting atmosphere that helps provide never-marrieds with the right environment for growth and addresses the central issues just described.

**Subgroup—"Never-Married with Children."** The profile of "never-marrieds" would be incomplete without adding information about an important emerging subgroup: never-married with children. Over the last three decades, the birth rate among never-marrieds has climbed dramatically. In 1960, one in twenty births was to an unwed mother. By 1990, that rate was one in four! [10]

Never-married parenthood mostly falls to the mother rather than to the father. Economic hardship, inadequate housing, and difficulty in pursuing further education or job training all add a unique slant to the challenges of the never-married with children. They often lack a positive environment where their children can receive support and they themselves can develop healthy friendships with other adults.

Never-married mothers and their children do not always feel comfortable in either never-married group activities (because the others have no children), or single parent activities (because the others have all been married and divorced). But as a supportive institution, the church has the opportunity to offer crucial structure and identity for the life-style concerns of this subgroup.

---

*Only about one-quarter of all [never-married] mothers and three-quarters of all divorced or separated mothers are awarded child support. Even then, only about half of these women actually receive what is legally due them. The average amount a mother received in 1989 was under $3,000.* [11]

---

## 2. Divorced

*Description:* Like it or not, divorce has become part of the American way of life. Current statistics indicate that only one out of every two marriages is likely to survive. According to Barna's research, today over 16 million Americans are currently divorced. More divorced persons live in metropolitan areas than in rural towns. More than 3 million divorced women are raising children alone, while another 1.3 million women are separated and parenting alone.[12]

---

*I read the other day that there are 1,250,000 new divorces every year in the United States. That means 2,500,000 husbands and wives go through the divorce experience annually. If we add two children to each divorce, our number would climb to 5,000,000 mothers, fathers and children involved in a divorce each year. Add two sets of parents (grandparents) and the number climbs to 10,000,000 primary family members who are affected by divorce. Ten million! Can you name any other national disaster that affects more lives each year?*
—Jim Smoke[13]

---

The divorced represent a vast variety of socioeconomic groups and display an assorted array of resulting emotional, financial, and spiritual implications in their lives. They do, however, all share the traumatic experience of crisis and change in the family unit which impacts everyone and everything connected to the situation. The majority of the divorced are also parents, so they too share the difficult struggles of single parenthood

# Today's Single Adults

## Their Ages . . .

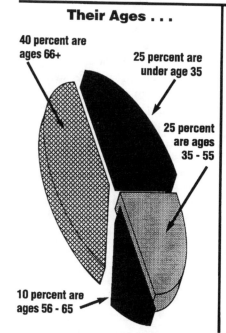

40 percent are ages 66+

25 percent are under age 35

25 percent are ages 35 - 55

10 percent are ages 56 - 65

## Their Marital Status . . .

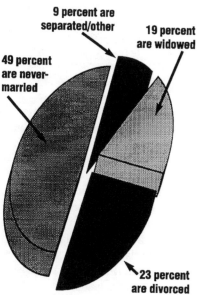

9 percent are separated/other

19 percent are widowed

49 percent are never-married

23 percent are divorced

**SINGLE PERSON HOUSEHOLDS CONTINUE TO INCREASE:** According to *New Realities of the American Family*, 25 percent of all U.S. households consist of just one person, up from 17 percent in 1970. And the raw mass of people living in them has more than doubled, soaring from 11 million then to over 23 million now.

**SOURCES:** *Newsweek*, March 1, 1993, page 70; *New Realities of the American Family* by Dennis A. Ahlburg and Carol J. De Vita (Washington, D.C.: Population Reference Bureau, Inc., August 1992) page 6; *Marital Status and Living Arrangements: March 1992* by Arlene F. Saluter, U.S. Department of Commerce, Bureau of the Census.

(both custodial and noncustodial).

Divorce forces most people to face a total re-invention of existence—including relationships, life-style, parenting techniques, financial security, and faith in God. Sometimes it results in a geographical move, estrangement from family, and shipwrecked self-esteem. Newly-divorced people often share a kinship of pain and brokenness which can facilitate mutual support.

---

*One of the earliest hurdles to be faced in a divorce is the struggle of letting go of the many things that were a part of the marriage experience. Divorce brings a vast number of changes into the lives of those involved. . . . Divorce forces people to change. Change involves letting go of old things and accepting new things. Every life is maintained by various support systems. We grow and depend upon mental, physical, social and spiritual structures for our support. When any of these structures is weakened, we become confused, disoriented, frustrated, insecure, or uncertain. Divorce introduces numerous changes in each of these four areas.* —JIM SMOKE[14]

---

Two-thirds of today's divorced adults want a close relationship with God. Nearly 70 percent of divorced people say they have made a "personal commitment to Jesus Christ that is still important" in their lives. This is in contrast to never-marrieds, where only 54 percent report a personal commitment.[15] This data reveals that the majority of divorced people view religious beliefs favorably as a source of support and spiritual guidance.

What is your church's doctrinal position concerning divorce and remarriage? The "theology of divorce" your church or denomination espouses will impact how welcome the divorced feel when they attend or participate.

► See the bibliography, page 190, for resource ideas regarding both adult and children's divorce recovery.

---

*If ever there was a stigma attached to singleness, the divorced single carries the lion's share. Many divorced Christians know the stigma well and report that they feel like the 'lepers' of the church. Since biblical days, divorce has been shunned and decried as an activity of the faithless. . . . [but] those whose marriages have ended still deserve their congregation's continued love and support.* —SHERON PATTERSON[16]

---

*Key issues.* This research information about the divorced, coupled with ministry experience involving this group, have helped clarify several common needs the church should recognize.

• *Divorce recovery.* Judith Wallerstein, author of *Second Chances: Men, Women, and Children a Decade after Divorce*, has written that her surveys with divorced people reveal an average of two and a half to three years of necessary "recovery time" for adults after the crisis[17] (given no complicating dysfunction such as alcohol or abuse). Many divorced move ahead with re-focus and adjustment more expeditiously with the help of recovery support group experiences. This setting can also offer guidelines about healthy relationship dynamics.

In addition, divorce recovery for children is just as vital. New curricula and resources for children's divorce recovery programs are now becoming available. ◄

• *Single-parent issues.* Divorce impacts the entire family. Newly-single parents must learn how to parent alone effectively, or in a custodial/noncustodial co-parenting situation. Single-parent support groups give attenders a chance to share concerns and gain new information about healthy single-parent family dynamics.

In addition, dealing with financial concerns and learning effective budgeting techniques become urgent issues for single parents. According to 1992 national statistics, the median income of female-headed households with no husband present was less than half ($18,069) of the traditional family's income.[18] Child support payments are not enough to bring many single-parent families above the poverty line.

• *Remarriage/stepfamily dynamics.* Stepfamily ministry is closely related to singles ministry, because many of the single parents in your group will remarry.

Dick Dunn, author and director of the stepfamily ministry at Roswell United Methodist Church in Roswell, Georgia, reports that a new stepfamily requires four to seven years together to feel like a "normal family." However, most stepfamily divorces occur within their first one to three years. Education about healthy relationships, stepfamily systems, conflict resolution, and support from other stepfamilies is crucial for "blended families" to succeed.[19]

*What the church can offer.* The church can provide divorce support groups and courses on the key issues divorced people face. In addition, acceptance can be communicated by integrating these single adults into all phases of church life, providing opportunities for service to others.

*Subgroup—"Separated."* A subgroup to highlight here is the separated. Those who comprise this group present a difficult area of ministry. This is a painful way to live, too—separated individuals often describe their lives with the term "split identity" (being both married and single).

Many separated people do not feel they belong with a group of marrieds. But neither do they feel comfortable in a singles group, because it might give the impression they are "looking" before their divorce has become final, or before they have ultimately decided whether they will, in fact, divorce.

The church can offer the separated a safe place to serve others and to grow spiritually as they sort out their troubling marriage concerns. Separated people can benefit from healthy relationship education and crisis support groups as they work to clarify their future.

### 3. Widowed

*Description.* The U.S. Bureau of the Census has reported that 72 percent of all widowed persons in our country are over 65 years old. Seventeen percent of those between 55-64 are widowed. Widowed people ages 20-54 comprise only about 10 percent of the total widowed population.[20]

The implication of these statistics is that the majority of widowed persons who may attend your singles activities will likely be older adults. And that number will keep increasing in the future. This striking demographic swing due to the aging population of our country will impact every singles ministry outreach in North America.

Since 1985 there have been more people age 65 and over than those 18 and younger. By 2025, Americans over 65 will outnumber teenagers by more than two to one—and most of them will be single or single again.[21]

---

*Twelve percent of American women, and 3% of American men, survive their spouses and remain unmarried. About one-quarter of all Americans ages 65-74 and about half of all Americans over age 75 are widows. They total almost 14 million Americans.* —GEORGE BARNA[22]

---

How much do you know about the older adult lifestyle of today? Traditionally, the elderly were cared for within the context of their extended families. But today's older adults are generally expected to take care of themselves. They depend more on their retirement savings and own housing than on their grown

▶ Refer to the bibliography, page 190, for excellent resources that can equip you for ministry with the various groups of single adults.

children. Government benefits have raised their standard of living, in some cases dramatically, over the last fifty years. They can expect to live longer, enjoy more leisure time, and invest more energy in volunteer capacities than any other population segment.

Those in singles ministry are entitled to think of the widowed as an unusually supportive constituency for the church. About half of America's widows believe that Christianity imparts more influence in our country today than it did five years ago, and that the church is sensitive to their needs.[23] While this may not hold true in years to come (due to the wave of unchurched, secularized "baby boomers" who will be moving into the older adult age group), it offers current singles groups a prime opportunity to provide significant ministry for widowed adults.

*Key issues.* What are key issues for the widowed? We suggest the following as "connecting points" between widowed adults and the church.

• *Grief recovery.* The loss of a spouse requires emotional, financial, social, and often spiritual re-orientation for the widowed. Dealing with the loss through grief support groups or a support network is integral to the healing process.

• *Fellowship opportunities.* While most widowed persons may display a busy schedule, they also desire means for cultivating new acquaintances and friendships. Less frequently included in the activities of their married friends, the widowed find a common bond with one another in their grief experience.

• *Remarriage preparation.* For those who are open to the possibility, remarriage education and support are vital.

• *Aging issues.* For the widowed who are seniors, learning the art of "successful aging" can add zest and satisfaction to the later years. Health self-care, good nutrition, exercise, travel, volunteerism, learning experiences, and spiritual

growth are all issue the church can help older singles explore. ◀

*What the church can offer.* The church can provide friendship, grief support groups, and opportunities for growth, service, and networking.

## What Is the Right Attitude?

To reiterate the premise of this chapter, how you view the single adults in your church and community directly impacts the effectiveness of your ministry and who attends the events.

### Singles are valuable people

"Poor people!" one minister lamented about the single adults in his congregation. "They're destined to go through at least part of their lives as half-persons, being not married and all. It's the least our church can do to help pull them together. You know misery probably loves company!"

Do you view the single adults around you as second-class citizens—or do you see them as valuable human beings with gifts, abilities, and talents? Have you read about, spent time with, and listened to a variety of single adults enough to understand their views of the world? Being divorced, never-married, separated, or widowed is not, and should not be, the primary definition of any person's identity. A person's marital status is ultimately only one attribute of his or her life. Many other qualities, issues, and characteristics link that person to God and others on the most fundamental level.

### Singles face struggles common to all

One central argument for singles ministry is that it helps people deal with the unique challenges and transitions of the single life. But at the core of those unique challenges are the same basic struggles everyone faces—struggles with relationships, parenting, faith issues, finances,

(continued on page 36)

## Single Adults and Some Issues They Face

| SINGLE ADULT CATEGORY (AGES 20+) | KEY ISSUES TO ADDRESS | WHAT THE CHURCH CAN OFFER |
|---|---|---|
| **Never-married**<br>• More than half are 18-24.<br>• 31% are 25-34.<br>• Nearly 40% are over 30.<br>• Average age is rising.<br>• Over half of those under age 30 live with their parents. | • Changing sexual values *(Nearly 80% have had a sexual relationship.)*<br>• Career, income, and possessions *(Personal happiness and self-fulfillment are high priorities.)*<br>• Death of a dream (and related grief) *(Many over 30 are dealing with the painful prospect of never having a mate or children.)* | • A place to form healthy adult relationships<br>• An accepting atmosphere that fosters growth and a sense of belonging within the church family<br>• Dialogue and instruction on the key issues |
| ***Subgroup: Never-married with children***<br>• In 1960, one in twenty births was to an unwed mother. By 1990, that rate was one in four. | • Single-parenting issues<br>• Grief<br>• Economic hardships<br>• Inadequate housing | • Support, structure, and identity for life-style concerns |
| **Divorced**<br>• Only one out of every two marriages is likely to survive.<br>• Over 16 million Americans are currently divorced.<br>• More than 3 million divorced women are raising children alone; another 1.3 million women are separated and parenting alone.<br>• Two-thirds of today's divorced adults want a close relationship with God. *(Nearly 70% say they have made a "personal commitment to Jesus Christ that is still important" in their lives.)* | • Divorce recovery *(Average "recovery time"—without complicating dysfunction such as alcohol or abuse—is 2 1/2 to 3 years.)*<br>• Remarriage/stepfamily dynamics<br>• Single-parenting skills<br>• Managing finances | • Education about healthy relationships, stepfamily systems, conflict resolution<br>• Support from other stepfamilies *(crucial for "blended families" to succeed)*<br>• Opportunities for significant involvement and service to others<br>• Inclusion in all phases of church life and adult education<br>• Acceptance in worship through single-sensitive sermon illustrations and prayers<br>• Single/grief/divorce support groups |
| ***Subgroup: Separated***<br>• Often describe their lives as "split identity" (being both married and single). | • Healthy relationship education<br>• Counseling referrals<br>• Connections with others in a similar situation for friendship and support<br>• Relationship clarification<br>• Temporary crisis counseling, housing, financial aid | •Acceptance, crisis counseling, temporary housing, and financial aid while sorting out troubling marriage/parenting concerns<br>• Opportunities to serve others<br>• Input for spiritual growth<br>• Emotional support and encouragement in clarifying the future<br>• Help in developing healthy relationships |
| **Widowed**<br>• 72% in U.S.A. are 65 years old.<br>• 17% of those between 55-64 are widowed.<br>• Only about 10% of widowed are ages 20-54.<br>• Since 1985 more people are age 65 and older than 18 and younger.<br>• By 2025, Americans over 65 will outnumber teenagers by more than two to one; most will be single or single again.<br>• They can expect to live longer, enjoy more leisure time, and invest more energy in volunteer capacities than any other population segment. | • Grief recovery *(They need emotional, financial, social, and often spiritual re-orientation.)*<br>• Fellowship opportunities *(The may display a busy schedule, but want to make new friendships.)*<br>• Remarriage preparation *(For those widowed who are open to the possibility, remarriage education and support are vital.)*<br>• Aging issues *(Widowed seniors can add zest and satisfaction to later years by learning the art of "successful aging.")* | • Friendship/networking with other widowed persons<br>• Grief support groups<br>• "Arm and Hammer" ministry *(Connect those who live alone with volunteer handypersons.)*<br>• Lifelong learning opportunities *(seminars, workshops, classes)*<br>• Spiritual growth/Bible study<br>• For widowed seniors, connections with health care resources, "Meals on Wheels," community senior center<br>• Single older adult activities |

career, politics, emotional health, and family. The key to successful singles ministry is responding to those deep, basic struggles within single adults with respect, dignity, and hope.

At a monthly church singles event, a haggard-looking, middle-aged woman edged into the fellowship hall where nearly two hundred laughing, talking people were involved in an icebreaker activity. "I'm here for the, well, the singles event," she mumbled to the chairperson.

"You're in the right place!" the chairperson answered.

"Oh, no!" the woman said as she looked at the animated group. "I mean I'm here to be with the—" she lowered her voice to a whisper, "the *divorced* people!"

Her eyes widened in disbelief as the chairperson said cheerfully, "These are divorced people!"

"But it couldn't be!" she gasped. "Why, they're having so much *fun!*"

**Single life is acceptable**

Some single adults think of themselves as handicapped for life. They feel surrounded and overwhelmed by the pressure of the married world. But the single ministry in today's church is responsible to manifest the premise that *single life is an acceptable, legitimate lifestyle, and to welcome, affirm, and support single persons as unique and special individuals.* The healing and wholeness this brings is at the heart of successful singles ministry. We are called to do the transforming, validating work of Christ amid the world's debilitating message that nonconformity is synonymous with failure.

This mission is a part of the church's task as a whole as it reaches out to a needy world. Singles ministry is a targeted area of that outreach, specially designed to address the journey and challenges of the single life.

▶ Resource 5, "Image Inventory," page 39, contains five questions about your image of single adults. Use it to prompt discussion with others in your church as you prepare to begin a singles ministry.

*Perhaps our most frequent mistake in evangelism is to begin where we are, with our interests, rather than where they [newcomers to the church] are. . . .We can begin where they are—even their self-interest—trusting that, in God's good time, their involvement with the Christian message, fellowship, and service will draw them out of mere self-interest into a new life, new relationships, and new lifestyle.*
—GEORGE HUNTER[24]

## IMAGE, IMAGE, IMAGE!

Someone once said, "What you radiate is what you attract." That is so true when it comes to building an effective ministry. Image is a theme which will surface throughout subsequent chapters in this book. The image your singles ministry has (or will have, if you are just getting started) is one of the most important factors you must consider as you forge a singles program. ◀

### Congregation's image of single adults

If in fact you want to attract sharp, growing single adults to your group, then your singles ministry should be viewed as a place led by and filled with bright, capable, creative adults who are living life to its fullest. This does not mean that you will seek to exclude the more lonely, hurting people. But it does mean that you need to be very intentional about the dominant image of your group. If you only have the more needy, struggling singles, then your group will develop that image. However, if you pursue the healthier person, you will attract both types. This image helps legitimize the healthy single life-style to the rest of the church. (Remember: *What you radiate is what you attract.*)

Accordingly, the activities you plan for the singles ministry should enhance this positive, healthy image, rather than reinforce the old myths and stereotypes about the single life. For example, if the image in your community or church is that singles party all the time, it might be best not to schedule a street party on the church parking lot!

Consider the following *seven ways to change your church's attitude toward—and improve their image of—single adults.*

1. Provide singles ministry information and positive support from the pulpit by the pastor.

2. Encourage the placement of single adults in leadership positions throughout the congregation.

3. Encourage single adults to give testimonies in the worship service or at church meetings, explaining how God has ministered to them through the church.

4. Include articles in the church newsletter and Sunday bulletin with demographic information about the community's single adults, a profile of the adult singles who attend your church, or articles featuring single adults who have made a difference in your church or community.

5. Initiate programs or conversations with all church boards and committees, providing information about the unique ministry opportunity single adults offer.

6. Help single adults focus on becoming part of the church's agenda and vision. Discourage any negative attitudes or complaining.

7. Be patient and prayerful. Attitudes don't change overnight. Focus on being consistent with reeducating the congregation, and together with the adult singles set the best example you can for faithful church service.

---

*Changing people's habits and way of thinking is like writing your instructions in the snow during a snowstorm. Every twenty minutes you must rewrite your instructions. Only with constant repetition will you create change.*
—DONALD L. DEWAR[25]

---

### Single adults' self-image

How the singles view *themselves* is at the heart of the "image" department. The biblical base for their personal self-image should be the scriptural truth that we each find our wholeness in Christ. If the single adults in your group seem to huddle together with a "poor us" attitude, no one will want to become part of the program. If, however, the singles feel good about themselves as healthy, growing individuals, they will project an appealing image. The church is called to be at the forefront of pointing the way toward a fulfilling life, whether single or married.

---

## Singleness Can Be a Gift

"An unfortunate reality that accompanies being single again is the feeling that we are now somehow less worthwhile than we were before and that we can only be restored to wholeness if replacements for our ex-spouses come into our lives. . . . Did you know, though, that God says singleness can be a gift? When Jesus' disciples heard His teachings on adultery and decided 'it is better not to marry,' He said, 'Not everyone can accept this word, but only those to whom it has been given' (Matt. 19:10, 11). Later in the New Testament, the apostle Paul referred to his singleness as a 'gift from God' (I Cor. 7:7).

"A gift? That's right! We can consider our state of life as a gift of freedom. That means we can choose to grow. We are not destined to be second best. We don't need to harbor resentment. God sees us as whole! And because He sees us that way, we can be free from all the other voices which attempt to make us bitter and angry and discontented." —Terry Hershey[26]

This healthy self-image of the participants in the singles program will be enhanced by the types of events, workshops, activities, study groups, and Bible study opportunities you incorporate into the schedule. Will your programs and activities be primarily problem-oriented, or will you also plan growth-oriented events? Divorce recovery seminars, twelve-step programs, and grief groups are all good—but many singles are ready for upbeat, personal growth opportunities and a challenge to move ahead with life. ◄

▶ Resource 6, "Famous Singles," page 41, is a quiz/mixer which emphasizes the fact that singles can make a difference in the world today.

## TOOLS TO HELP YOU

The resources on the following pages will help you and others in your church develop a healthy attitude toward singles and your singles ministry.

• **Resource 5, "Image Inventory"** *(Discussion Guide)* What is your attitude toward single adults? Use Resource 5 as a discussion guide as you prepare to begin a singles ministry. By uncovering your own attitudes and assumptions about singleness, you can find ways to inform and grow in your ability to minister to and with this important part of our population.

• **Resource 6, "Famous Singles"** *(Quiz/Mixer)* This great tool can help you emphasize the fact that singles can and do make a difference in the world. Use it with the leadership of your church as you begin to help them understand the vital role single adults can play in the life of the church and community. This quiz can help people overcome negative stereotypes, attitudes, and images they may have about single adults. Or use it for a retreat, conference, class, or study with your single adults. It will stimulate the thinking of single adults concerning their potential for achievement.

*Instructions for "Famous Singles"* Divide your group into teams of two. Then pass out copies of the quiz and see who can come up with the most correct match-ups in ten minutes. Following the allotted time, have the participants share a significant goal they feel God might want them to accomplish during this year, during the next five years, or during their lifetime, and what they are doing now—or could begin doing—to help reach that accomplishment or goal.

*Answers to "Famous Singles"* A–35; B–9; C–11; D–34; E–1; F–39; G–12; H–33; I–32; J–6; K–31; L–10; M–7; N–5; O–3; P–14; Q–23; R–13; S–2; T–20; U–22; V–25; W–28; X–21; Y–29; Z–38; a–30; b–37; c–36; d–26; e–19; f–18; g–27; h–8; i–17; j–24; k–15; l–4; m–16; n–40

# IMAGE INVENTORY

**Church** _____ **Date** _____

Discuss the following questions with others in your church as you prepare to begin a singles ministry.

**1. Why do you want to start a singles ministry at your church?** *(Pastor's request, personal interest or need as a single adult, etc.? Please specify.)*

**2. Who or what has helped shape your "image" of single adulthood?** *(Church doctrinal position, media, family history, single friends, personal experience, reading and study, etc.?)*

**3. Has your image of single adults been positive or negative? Why?**

*(continued)*

4. After reading the information about the never-married, the divorced, and the widowed in Chapter 2 of *Starting a Single Adult Ministry,* how have your perceptions changed—if at all—regarding these three types of singles?

Never-Married:

Divorced:

Widowed:

5. What intentional ways have been used in your church to perpetuate a positive image of single adults? *(The pulpit, the church newsletter, the singles themselves, other means?)*

6. What avenues could your church, staff, and singles use to be more intentional?

7. What single adult activities or program ideas for your church come to mind after your discussion of the above questions?

8. What will be your next step?

# FAMOUS SINGLES

Many single adults have and are making a difference in the world. See how many of the following single adults and accomplishments you can match in ten minutes.

## SINGLE ADULTS

A. ____ Hans Christian Andersen
B. ____ Virginia Apgar
C. ____ Stephen F. Austin
D. ____ Frank Ball
E. ____ Clara Barton
F. ____ Katharine Lee Bates
G. ____ Emily Bissel
H. ____ Elizabeth Blow
I. ____ Dietrich Bonhoeffer
J. ____ Phillips Brooks
K. ____ Jerry Brown
L. ____ James Buchanan
M. ____ Eva Burrows
N. ____ Annie Jump Cannon
O. ____ Charlotte Elliott
P. ____ Fanny Farmer
Q. ____ Edward Gibbon
R. ____ Sarah Josepha Hale
S. ____ Dag Hammarskjold
T. ____ George F. Handel
U. ____ Grace Hooper
V. ____ J. Edgar Hoover
W. ____ Johns Hopkins
X. ____ Washington Irving
Y. ____ John Paul Jones
Z. ____ Helen Keller
a. ____ Edward Koch
b. ____ S.H. Kress
c. ____ Emma Lazarus
d. ____ James Clark McReynolds
e. ____ Julia Morgan
f. ____ Sam Rayburn
g. ____ Cecil Rhodes
h. ____ William Scholl
i. ____ Adam Smith
j. ____ Adlai Stevenson
k. ____ Ida Tarbell
l. ____ Samuel J. Tilden
m. ____ Raoul Wallenberg
n. ____ Anna Warner

## ACCOMPLISHMENTS

1. Founded the American Red Cross
2. A secretary-general of the U.N.
3. Wrote the hymn "Just as I Am"
4. Broke up Boss Tweed's gang
5. Named 350,000 stars
6. Wrote "O Little Town of Bethlehem"
7. General of the Salvation Army
8. Pioneered research in foot care
9. Raised millions for the March of Dimes
10. A never-married U.S. President
11. First president of Texas
12. Developed Christmas Seals
13. Lobbied for a national Thanksgiving Day
14. Developed a major U.S. cookbook
15. Muckraker who exposed Standard Oil
16. Rescued thousands of Jews from Nazis
17. Economist; wrote *Wealth of Nations*
18. A Speaker for U.S. House of Representatives
19. Architect; designed the Hearst Castle
20. Composed "The Messiah"
21. U.N. ambassador; created Rip Van Winkle
22. A major developer of the computer
23. Wrote *The Decline and Fall of the Roman Empire*
24. U.N. ambassador; ran twice for U.S. Presidency
25. Headed the FBI
26. Served on Supreme Court for 26 years
27. Gold and diamond miner who endowed scholarships
28. Endowed Baltimore University
29. Said, "I have not yet begun to fight"
30. Was bachelor mayor of New York City
31. Was bachelor governor of California
32. Theologian who plotted Hitler's death
33. Opened first kindergarten in the U.S.
34. Developed fruit jars for home canning
35. Wrote fairy tale classics
36. Wrote, "Give me your tired, your poor . . ."
37. Founded a department store chain
38. Reformed treatment of the blind
39. Wrote "America the Beautiful"
40. Wrote "Jesus Loves Me, This I Know"

Source: Adapted with permission from the book *A Singular Devotion*, by Harold Ivan Smith (Revell, 1990). Answers on page 38 of *Starting a Single Adult Ministry*.

# Nuts and Bolts
# of
# Getting Started

REPRODUCIBLE RESOURCES AT THE END OF THIS CHAPTER

When beginning a singles ministry, the first question is always the practical one: *What should we do first?*

If you have carefully considered Chapter 1, "Does Your Church Really Need a Single Adult Ministry?" and Chapter 2, "A Check-Up on Attitudes toward Single Adults," and are convinced your church could support and offer a good program, it's time to get started. Make sure, however, that you have finished the demographic research and "image check." Starting right the first time is much easier than going back and trying to revive a floundering singles ministry that was poorly conceived. When a church gains a reputation for having an unhealthy singles program, that reputation and image is usually hard to change.

## BEGIN WITH A DREAM TEAM

Begin with a small brainstorming team, also called a "dream team." To create the impetus you need for the ministry, invite at least five people to serve on this initial dream team. ◀

**Whom should you invite?**

Your first thought might be to put a notice in the Sunday church bulletin announcing that you will have a singles ministry brainstorming session, inviting anyone interested to come. While this approach is tolerable and no one who wants to come should be excluded, *you must recruit key people to serve on this team.* Carefully evaluate your choices, considering the following types of individuals.

*People with various perspectives.* Choose individuals with differing perspectives. They will help you identify a broader perspective of the needs and interests of the single adult community in your area and offer a wider diversity of ideas on what kind of programs, ministries, and outreaches to try. *Do not assume the people you most want on the dream team will automatically volunteer!*

*Positive people.* Avoid having a dream team of "complainers" who talk at length about the drawbacks of singleness, but don't know what they want for a ministry. Complainers often volunteer, but tend to use the brainstorming time as a "gripe session" and fail to be productive. However, people you have specifically invited to be on the dream team will understand they are included because they are respected for having worthwhile ideas and insights.

*"In-touch" people.* As much as possible, the people you invite should have their fingers on the heartbeat of the single adult population in your church and community. It is not required that they become involved in the singles programs which will eventually emerge from the brainstorming, but they should be able to offer ideas and suggestions on what is needed and how your church might effectively begin addressing those needs.

▶ Resource 7, "Dream Team Preparation," page 56, is a worksheet to guide you through the preparation necessary to cover all the bases described in this chapter.

---

## Being Sensitive to Non-Christians' Needs

**One of the most troubling perceptions of non-believers is that churches are insensitive to their needs. George Barna believes churches today have no excuse for perpetuating this tarnished image.**

**"Get to know the non-Christians in your area by spending time with them personally," Barna advises. "From a professional standpoint, you may wish to conduct occasional focus groups among the target groups you wish to reach. Listen to their fears, their anger, their anxieties, their assumptions related to churches. Accept their feelings and experiences at face value and create an outreach that responds to the barriers they perceive to exist."[1]**

***Non-Christians/unchurched.*** Include some persons on the dream team who are not Christians and who are not active churchgoers. If the church wishes to reach beyond the congregation, you must listen to the needs and wants of all different types of people. By thinking together with a variety of single adults, a clearer picture can be provided for the ministry's direction.

## Who should facilitate the brainstorming sessions?

You may be a great candidate for this job! If you do not feel comfortable as the potential facilitator, invite an objective person with few ties to your topic or agenda to focus the brainstorming. This could be someone with professional skills in this area such as a professor, teacher, or personnel director. You could go to the church's board of elders or administrative board. Or you may even invite someone who is not a member of your church. The key is to find someone who understands and can use brainstorming techniques. Make sure your facilitator is sensitive and sympathetic to issues and perspectives of the single life.

A staff member or pastor of your church could also be the facilitator. Having a pastor or staff on the dream team can help them develop a greater sense of ownership and support for the singles ministry, and establish a much needed link of communication.

However, having someone "official" on the team sometimes changes the group dynamics. Participants may be reluctant to share thoughts, instead acquiescing to the pastor's or staff's comments. If you choose to not include the pastor or a staff member on the dream team, keep them advised (either in writing or in person) of the team's conclusions and plans after each session.

NOTE: If you have been hired by your church specifically to work in singles ministry, it is acceptable for you to chair the initial dream team. But strive to prepare volunteer leaders for future team leadership.

## How should the facilitator prepare?

The team facilitator should prepare thoroughly before meeting with the group.

***Brush up on brainstorming.*** Your library and bookstores offer many books on the art of brainstorming, which is perhaps the best of all techniques for helping groups think creatively.

According to James L. Adams in *The Care and Feeding of Ideas*, the four rules of brainstorming are:

• Absolutely no evaluation or criticism.

• Any possible idea is acceptable, no matter what the quality.

• Come up with as many ideas as possible.

• Build upon other ideas.[2]

Brainstorming is important because of its tremendous *benefits*.

---

## Stimulate Creativity in Your Dream Team

**Three books that can stimulate creativity for your dream team are:**

• ***A Whack on the Side of the Head: How You Can Be More Creative*** by Roger Von Oech (New York: Warner Books, 1990).

• ***Wishcraft: How to Get What You Really Want*** by Barbara Sher (New York: Viking Press, 1979).

• ***A Kick in the Seat of the Pants*** by Roger Von Oech (New York: Harper and Row, 1986).

• It helps identify the issues and needs from a broader perspective.

• It spreads ownership of ideas and enthusiasm throughout the group.

• It lets those from differing viewpoints, including the pragmatist and the visionary, all give uncriticized, equal input.

• It expands the group vision.

• It motivates the group to want to move beyond the status quo.

***Understand the facilitator's job.*** The facilitator has the following responsibilities:

• Encourage, assist, and promote the group members to think without limits.

• Gently urge group members to explore, to dream, to consider.

• Help group members piggyback and dovetail their own and others' ideas.

***Lay aside personal agenda.*** Before the group ever convenes, the facilitator must try to lay aside any personal, preconceived agenda concerning future singles activities. He or she should prepare to listen carefully to team participants and be ready to encourage them to search, probe, and investigate risk or hindrances. The facilitator's opportunity to provide input will come when the group organizes and defines the ideas born through the brainstorming.

***Collect resources.*** Depending on the dream team members' interests and wishes, you may want to provide several books on single adult ministry, divorce recovery ministry, single parent ministry, and young adult ministry for them to peruse before you meet. Outside reading may enhance their brainstorming capabilities with new viewpoints. ◀

Remember, however, that what works in one church may not work in another. Your dream team must not simply adopt another church's ministry targets, purpose statement, and programs. Instead, the goal is to create a unique and accurate assessment of your own situation,

▶ Refer to the guideline sheet, "How to Hold Effective Meetings," page 184, in the Appendix.

▶ See the bibliography, page 190, for recommended resources.

hopes, and opportunities.

*Call a meeting. Arrange to meet with the dream team at a mutually convenient time and place.* Establish both the starting and ending time of the meeting so the dream team members understand the time commitment you ask. Set up the seating area in your meeting location so the chairs are in a circle, or around a table so all can see each other. If you are meeting at the church, arrange child care in a nearby classroom for team members' children, if needed.

To prepare for the meeting, take the worksheets you've completed from Chapters 1 and 2, and make copies for each team member. These will provide the team with information about single adults in your congregation and community. ◀

***Prepare an agenda.*** The three primary tasks on the agenda of the dream team are:

***1. Brainstorm*** a list of each of the following things:

• Every conceivable issue and topic relevant to single adults in your church, your town, and your area.

• Every local resource available to help a singles program, including people, programs, places.

• Every possible (or seemingly impossible!) way to reach single adults in your community or area.

***2. Identify and prioritize*** from that list a few key areas of single adult ministry in which your church should become involved. Establish priorities. Since you will be unable to accomplish everything at once, determine those few places where you want to begin and build first.

***3. Create a definition*** of your single ministry's purpose.

**What should the agenda include?**

Take a closer look at each agenda task.

***1. Brainstorm a list of issues, topics,***

*resources, and ideas.* Encourage the dream team to let ideas and observations flow. Emphasize that no comment is ridiculous—every perspective should be considered. For a springboard, use the data you have gathered on worksheets from Chapter 1. Remember, the ideas that initially seem most irrelevant often point to something the group is overlooking. Brainstorming is simply a method of getting the ideas out of your heads and hearts and in front of the group. Declare a moratorium on judging any ideas until all ideas have been expressed.

To get started, ask the team:

• *What issues (either problem-oriented or growth-oriented) are important to the single adults you know?*

• *Ideally, what would you like to see happen for and with single adults in our church? In our community?*

As your team brainstorms, they'll find it helpful if all the ideas are written on a flip chart. As each page is filled with suggestions and observations, hang it on the wall so everyone can see it. Make sure you (or someone you designate) also keeps good notes of this session for reference at future meetings.

*2. Identify key areas of single adult ministry in which your church should be involved.* This step comes after all possible comments, suggestions, and observations have been compiled. It is likely that this task may take place at your second dream team session.

Finding the most effective ministry areas to undertake may be a challenging job for your team. Should you start a ministry to single parents? to the newly divorced? to young adults? to the never married? a Sunday morning class? Will your programs focus on discipleship or be outreach-oriented? Why?

Narrow your fields. Although you may have dozens of ideas, they can probably be organized into three to five basic categories. Again, record these on a flip chart or large sheets of paper visible to everyone.

After you categorizing ideas, rank them according to their priority in each category. Finally, let the group scan the brainstorming lists and ask these questions:

• *Is anyone else in the community/ town/city already doing this?*

• *What can we create without unnecessarily duplicating activities which may already exist?*

• *Why is this something that's important for our church to do?*

## How Much Brainstorming Time Do You Need?

**The size of your dream team, the size of your church, and the size of your community all impact the extensiveness of your brainstorming.** No brainstorming session should last more than two hours, unless you have a weekend retreat in which scheduling is flexible and the team agrees to keep rolling. You will probably need more than one session to suggest and develop ideas, to categorize, define, and prioritize, and to spread the ownership of your task among the group.

**But how many meetings are necessary to complete these three agenda tasks?** Some groups have found it best to tackle only one agenda task per meeting. For example, you may even need two meetings per task to focus and hone. Other groups cover the territory more briskly. At the end of this chapter you'll find a sample "Dream Team Agenda." This will help you see how to set up each dream team meeting to run effectively and productively.

**Always remember a dream team will lose interest, focus, and unity if you belabor points, or spend meeting time complaining about past failures or what the church lacks.** Work positively, efficiently, and quickly. Be task-oriented.

---

## Dream Team Steps Really Work!

**The single adult ministry of First Presbyterian Church of Aurora, Illinois, had shrunk from an average attendance of 200 to 15. By returning to these basic steps of brainstorming, categorizing, prioritizing, and defining, they reestablished a sense of vision for a singles ministry. This process helped redefine goals, establish direction, and provide leadership accountability. Within six months, the singles ministry began growing consistently again on a weekly basis.**

---

Above all, focus your target toward the needs of single persons who are moving toward, and committed to, personal growth. Hopefully, your dream team members themselves fit this description. Many singles ministries struggle because they are aimed only at the lonely, depressed, and down-and-out. As a result, they unconsciously convey that image to the church and community.

Meeting the needs of the hurting and broken single adults of your community is vital. But your singles ministry should focus on getting people back on their feet and helping them stay there.

Otherwise, you will carry the reputation as a group of single adults who are perpetually needy and wounded. And as mentioned earlier, this unhealthy image is difficult to change later.

*3. Defining the purpose of your singles ministry is the dream team's last major task.* Without a specific purpose, your singles ministry may become an indistinct body of unrelated activities and a group lacking specific direction. A concise purpose statement helps you maintain focus. A purpose statement should answer the question, "Why does our singles ministry exist?" Your purpose statement should be concise and easy for your ministry participants to understand and articulate.

A weak or nonexistent purpose statement results in a group fitting these characteristics:

- *The ministry has no clear direction.*
- *The leadership cannot articulate the ministry focus.*
- *People don't know why the ministry exists.*

### DEVELOP A PURPOSE STATEMENT

In developing your own purpose statement, consider the following steps, caution, and sample purpose statements.

### Practical steps to creating a purpose statement

The following practical steps for creating a purpose statement are adapted from *Singles Ministry Resources Notebook* .[3]

---

## What to Do between Dream Team Meetings

**After your dream team has met for the first time, encourage the dream team members to informally interview as many single adults as possible before your next meeting.** This will help you discover what others think is needed for single adult programming by the church, and what the key ingredients for a singles ministry should be. This also enhances and informs the dream team's focus and keeps team members in touch with the needs of single adults in your area.

**These conversations are also a type of low-key recruiting for your singles ministry.** When your group begins to hold events, you can return to those single adults and invite them to be a part of what has been created with their input.

**1. Make sure it is easy to understand!** Do not make the purpose statement long and complex. Do not use big words no one can understand. Also, try to stay away from "church" language. For example, avoid words like "redeeming," "fellowship," or phrases like "share the Gospel." Instead, try words like "lovable," "friendship," and "telling people about Jesus Christ." Using plain language makes your purpose statement "user-friendly" to unchurched newcomers.

**2. Make sure it is your purpose!** You may be tempted to copy someone else's statement that you like. However, your ministry is in a different setting and you are different people. Write your own statement accordingly.

**3. Make sure you believe it!** Don't use a statement just because it sounds good. Make sure you understand and believe it.

**4. Make sure it is compatible with the overall mission and vision of your senior pastor and church leadership!** This is crucial to insure their support. ▶

**5. Change it when necessary!** Don't feel like you can never change your statement. It is meant to serve you, not box you in. When desire for a new direction surfaces, reword your statement.

**Caution**

If you wish to list specific goals or objectives which are related to the purpose statement, do so. But don't overshadow a simply-worded purpose statement with a lengthy list of hopes and dreams. "Objectives" are the goals your ministry hopes to accomplish, and they should always feed back into and highlight the ministry's purpose.

The *danger* of adding a long list of objectives to your purpose statement is that it may set your group up for failure—especially if you list more than your group can ever hope to accomplish. A long list can also stifle the continued creativity of your leadership team because

◀ See "Building Your Ministry around a Statement of Purpose," page 51, for further information on how to make your ministry compatible with the church's mission and vision.

---

# Should You Give Your Singles Group a Special Name?

Many singles ministries choose to name their ministry in hopes of giving newcomers and participants an easy-to-remember point of reference.

**Here are some questions to answer as you brainstorm about coming up with a name for your group:**

**1. Does our suggested name accurately indicate our identity?**

For example, "First Church Singles" lets people know immediately the makeup of the group. So does "SoloFlight," "Singlepoint Ministries," and "Community Christian Singles." But using an acronym (like First Church S.A.M.) usually leaves most people guessing.

**2. Does our suggested name confuse our purpose?**

One church singles group named itself "Club Uno." After the group had done publicity throughout the community, the church office began regularly receiving calls from people who wanted to sign up for the "dating club."

**3. Does our suggested name unintentionally limit our target audience?**

"New Start" or "Reconnections" may be good names for groups involving divorced or widowed persons—but don't expect the never-marrieds in your church or community to assume you want them to attend.

**4. Have we received approval of our new name from the staff or senior pastor?**

Remember, your singles ministry needs to fit into the overall design and mission of your entire church purpose. Get feedback from the staff and pastor if you are choosing a new or unique name for your group.

everything seems already decided and planned. Aim for a balance and stick to the basics.

Your purpose statement should be reviewed periodically by the singles program leadership. Reshape and clarify it as needed. But always have a purpose statement available to help you check your direction and make sure your events line up with your planned direction.

### Sample purpose statements

These purpose statements from singles ministries across the country can give you ideas. Remember, your purpose statement should not be exactly like any of these; it should reflect *your* setting, *your* singles community, and the ministry goals of *your* dream team. It should be uniquely defined by *your* group.

**Church of the Open Door Singles Ministry**
**6421 45th Avenue North**
**Crystal, MN 55428**

We desire to look beyond our own existence to Jesus who meets our deepest needs for significance, value, security and healing.

We desire to be a group of people who choose to face the real pain of life rather than cover over it.

We desire to encourage each other with gifts of acceptance, grace, and commitment as we build a community of people.

We desire to break out of our own circle of safety and love those who are empty, lost and without hope.

**Church Street United Methodist Church**
**Singles Ministry**
**900 Henley at Main, P.O. Box 1303**
**Knoxville, TN 37901**

Our Purpose:

To affirm adults who are single by choice or by circumstance as whole, worthwhile people.

To reach out to all singles—never married, separated, divorced, and widowed—offering acceptance and community.

To offer many "ports of entry" and paths to supportive fellowship through a variety of activities, programs, classes, and mutual support groups.

To provide a wide array of opportunities for personal enrichment and service to others.

To be aware of and responsive to the individual needs of single adults in our midst.

To support and affirm single parents and their families.

To offer all this in a Christian community of grace.

**Willow Creek Community Church**
**"Focus" (Single Adult) Ministry**
**67 East Algonquin Road**
**South Barrington, IL 60010**

The Focus Ministry exists for the purpose of providing a Christ-centered arena in which single adults (ages 32-42) can be incorporated and involved in building the kingdom of God. This is done by assimilating new people into the church, discipling believers who are a part of the church, and building leaders who will make a commitment to building the kingdom of God.

**Willoughby Hills Friends Church**
**Single Friends Ministries**
**2846 S.O.M. Center**
**Willoughby Hills, OH 44094**

The purpose of Single Friends Ministries is to be an outreach arm of Willoughby Hills Friends Church that meets the needs of single adults of many ages and backgrounds.

Our ultimate goal is to see each person come into a personal relationship with Jesus Christ and be incorporated into the full life of the Church.

**Moody Church**
**"Single Focus" Ministry**
**1609 North La Salle Drive**
**Chicago, IL 60614**

Single Focus is a ministry of the Moody Church to Chicagoland Singles. We exist to put God's love into action by providing you with support, challenge, and opportunity in your pursuit of authentic living.

**St. Mark's United Methodist Church**
**Singles Ministry**
**740 N. 70th Street**
**Lincoln, NE 68505**

The Singles Ministry at St. Mark's is a multifaceted program for never-married, separated, divorced, and widowed adults from age twenty through retirement. The three-fold purpose of the ministry is:

• To provide settings in which mutual support systems and relationships can be built.

• To offer opportunities for personal growth toward wholeness.

• To encourage spiritual development.

The Singles Ministry operates within the context of the church as a whole, and seeks to help unmarried people develop an identity as an integral part within (not separate from) the entire faith community.

**Village Presbyterian Church (U.S.A.)**
**Mission Road at 67th Street**
**P.O. Box 8050**
**Prairie Village, KS 66208**

Village Singles Ministry is committed to meeting the spiritual, educational, psychological, recreational and social needs of single adults in an atmosphere of love and acceptance.

## SETBACKS—AND SUGGESTIONS

As you try to build a "launching pad" for a singles ministry, certain concerns may arise. Here are some of the most common questions churches and leaders have expressed.

### Questions and answers

*What shall I do if I can't find five people to be on an initial brainstorming team?* You probably need to reassess whether you need a singles ministry program. Consider spending the next six months to a year in singles "outreach." Pray and reach out to the single adults around you, befriending them and ministering to them in every way you can. Baby-sit for single parents, listen to those

---

# Building Your Ministry around a "Statement of Purpose"

The singles ministry can become an island within the total church ministry, off on its own. A healthy ministry will be vitally involved in the life of the total church body. Here is one way to incorporate your singles ministry into the broader mission of your church.

Study a copy of your church's "Statement of Purpose." Then design each week's major function around it. For example, here is the statement of purpose developed by the Skyline Wesleyan Church of Lemon Grove, California.

*As a dynamic church proclaiming the Word of God, we purpose to make disciples of Christ by:*

*1. Attracting and leading the unsaved to Jesus.*

*2. Encouraging Christians to consecrate themselves to God's purpose in their lives.*

*3. Providing a climate in which personal spiritual growth and worship occur.*

*4. Equipping believers for effective ministry to reach our city and beyond.*

The singles ministry of this church then focuses on one of the four statements each Sunday. The first Sunday of the month, they emphasize evangelism. The class lesson includes a warm evangelistic message. The group takes no offering, and no guests are asked to stand and give their names. They employ the use of drama and special music to focus on the message.

On the second Sunday, the theme is commitment and consecration. On the third Sunday, it's spiritual growth and nurture, and the fourth, service. As part of the class on the fourth Sunday, pre-selected singles stand and briefly tell about a ministry they're involved with (such as children's Sunday school, divorce recovery, missions, music). The leaders share new ministry opportunities and service possibilities with the group. Singles are challenged to give of themselves, and are provided specific suggestions for service.

This is one way to effectively build a strong singles ministry around the mission of your church.[4]

experiencing bereavement, divorce, or the loneliness of living alone. Invite them to church, socialize with them. (Remember that you do not have to have a "program" to have a "ministry" with the people around you. Ministry can be simply reaching out and touching the lives of people one person at a time.)

In six months to a year, reconsider whether or not you have cultivated enough individuals for a brainstorming team and a singles program.

As you implement "outreach," you will probably need to work on your church's attitude about single adults. Review the list of ways to improve your church's attitude (Chapter 2). Along with your senior pastor or church staff, develop ways to broaden the church perspective about single adults.

***Our church only has three single adults. Can we have a singles ministry?*** You may already have one if you have the true definition of "ministry" in mind. Ministry can exist with two or three people sitting across the table from each other, drinking coffee as they care, listen to each other, and support one another with prayer. Ministry is reaching out and caring for others in Christ's love, sharing joys and concerns, praying together, supporting each other.

No matter how many singles are in your small church or community, you can have this kind of ministry. For a singles program, though, you might check around for singles groups or events at a church with more single adults. The singles from your small church could attend those groups or programs together, thus keeping your fellowship while taking advantage of a larger church's singles program. You could also join other small churches for a community or regional ministry. ◀

Beware of confusing the definition of *ministry* with the definition of *programs*. Though churches sometimes use these

▶ See Chapter 11 for ideas especially for small churches.

words interchangeably, they have different meanings. Successful ministry is always the goal. Programs can help encourage ministry by providing a conducive setting, and by allowing ways to "quantify" the response of your effort (i.e., how many attended). But playing the "numbers" game (equating an event attended by a large number of people with "successful ministry") is a losing game. Keep your perspective.

***After our initial dream team met and identified two or three target areas, we planned six different events. Most of these events failed. What happened?*** One pitfall which can trip newly-launched singles programs is that the enthusiastic leaders plan too much too fast. In the beginning, a group should plan only one or two events at a time and carry them out with quality, excellence, and prayer. If you adhere to high standards, more events will develop. If your energy and volunteers are spread too thin, the fledgling program structure may collapse.

Note the difference between developing a program and developing a ministry. A few people can put together a lot of programs and invite plenty of speakers. But it takes time and care to spread the ownership and build many strong leaders who run the *ministry*—in contrast to many people attending programs run by a handful. If just a few leaders are doing it all, no commitment or ownership is expanded to others.

At Singlepoint Ministries of Ward Presbyterian Church, the leadership team stipulated that each leader could hold only one leadership role within the singles ministry. That provided the opportunity for many people to share the ownership of the ministry.

Attendance at your events is directly related to the breadth of leadership you have developed. Remember, most flourishing singles programs have taken the time and care to grow at a rate the leadership and planning could handle. One step at a time is the best strategy to sustain your program.

*How can we get our senior pastor to support our singles program?* Often single adults arrive at the senior pastor's office with their own program agenda in hand, asking the senior pastor to listen to and endorse their purpose without ever asking if it fits into the church's total vision of ministry. It appears they expect the pastor to put aside the overall vision for the church in order to accomplish the single adults' agenda. As a result, many senior pastors view singles groups as needy and demanding. And yet without the senior pastor's support and cooperation, a singles ministry will struggle, flounder, and often fail.

These steps can help you establish support and teamwork with the pastor:

*1. Schedule an appointment.* At the appointment, ask what pastoral vision and long-term goals exist for the church. Find out (and understand) what your pastor's hopes and dreams for the church really are.

*2. Ask your pastor.* How could a single adult ministry help achieve those goals for our church? Listen to your pastor's comments, and then offer your insight.

*3. Share your hope to form a brainstorming team.* Tell your pastor that the team's task would be to create a singles ministry purpose statement and to identify ministry areas for singles programs which would be in accord with the overall church purpose.

*4. Offer your pastor some books about singles ministry to look through.* One excellent resource for your pastor is the *Single Adult Ministries Journal*, a national, transdenominational publication which provides practical helps, ideas, and encouragement for those ministering to single adults. (*Single Adult Ministries*

*Journal* may be obtained by calling 1-800-487-4SAM, or by writing S.A.M. Journal, P.O. Box 62056, Colorado Springs, CO 80962-2056. Complimentary issues are available upon request.)

*5. Keep the pastor informed of your single adults events, and how they relate to the overall church vision or direction.* Regularly visit with your pastor and ask for input. Stay within the congregational vision for mission and ministry. ▶

## PLANNING YOUR FIRST EVENT

When a purpose statement is completed and the target audiences are established, the original dream team has completed its task. *The next step is to plan the first program or event.* WHO will this event be for? WHEN is a good time to schedule it? WHERE will it be held? HOW should it be publicized? WHAT is the purpose of the event?

You are now at an important moment of transition—putting thoughts into action. Remember that your original invitation to this group of people was only to serve on the brainstorming team. Whether or not any of them volunteer to help lead the first event is a different question. Express your appreciation to each of them, and make sure they have a dignified opportunity to either step aside or to continue with planning the first event. (Remember: *The only commitment you initially asked of them was to serve on the dream team. They should not be made to feel guilt at this point if they choose not to participate further.*)

Many times, however, the leadership for your first events will come from this initial dream team because of their enthusiasm for the project. The ownership of ideas is a powerful motivation for dream team members to move on into leadership of the actual events. This is another reason why you need to carefully select the original dream team—many of them

◀When your dream team has finished brainstorming, focusing, and preparing a purpose statement, record the results on Resource 9, "Dream Team Results," page 59. Then meet with the pastor personally and go over it together.

may become your first leaders.

After your dream team has completed its tasks, these are the next steps to take in planning the first event. ◄

▶ The steps given here for developing a first entry-level event are expanded upon in Chapter 4, complete with examples.

**1. Talk to each person who served on the initial dream team, and invite him/her to participate in a new dream team to plan the first event.**

If a person says no, accept the answer gracefully. Remember the person may want to just attend the first singles event and move into leadership later. If the answer is yes, welcome that person to the new team and discuss when it would be convenient to schedule a new team meeting.

**2. Add people to the team who represent the target group of single adults you would like to reach first.**

Think about the single adults who gave dream team members outside input throughout your initial brainstorming process. Invite a few dependable, positive people who fit the category of your target group to join the new team.

For example, if you're trying to reach single parents, include several single parents—both male and female, custodial and noncustodial—on your planning team. They'll help you understand how to make the event "user-friendly" for single parents.

▶ See Chapter 5, "Creating Quality Events," for guidelines in attending to event details.

**3. Establish a time and place for a meeting of the new dream team.**

Use the same protocol as when you set up the initial dream team meeting: provide child care if needed, have a circular seating arrangement, designate a facilitator or leader, and begin and end on time.

**4. At the meeting, evaluate the target areas established by the initial dream team and examine the purpose statement.**

Brainstorm on possible events to reach the target group. As you plan, keep an open mind about different possible types of events. Remember that single adults like larger events so they can meet new people; they also like smaller groups in order to get to know people better. They enjoy growing spiritually, relationally, intellectually, and emotionally.

After you've brainstormed, narrow your choices to a single event you agree on.

**5. After brainstorming comes "barn-raising."**

Barn-raising is putting concrete suggestions around a central idea or figuring out the specific needs for that event. What will it take for your team to make the event happen?

As you think through it, list every detail of creating the event—right down to napkins for the refreshments, signs for the doors on where to enter, and what kind of publicity will reach your target group. ◄

**6. Choose people who will be responsible for your barn-raising elements.**

Carefully review the list (as developed in step five above) carefully, and think about people and resources to help provide what you need. Team members can volunteer for their share of the responsibility. Together you may think of others with talents or abilities whom you can ask to contribute. For example, one of you may know someone who can generate the publicity brochure or flyer. Another may know someone who could provide the child care. Let your enthusiasm flow as you process what it will take to make the event happen. (Remember: *It is best if each person has only one responsibility at a time. This minimizes burnout and helps force you to get more people involved. If you do have more tasks than people available, share the load—and ownership—by distributing the responsibilities evenly among you.)*

## STAGING YOUR FIRST EVENT

The next two chapters have been carefully prepared to help you stage your first event.

### Chapter 4—"Points of Entry: Opening Doors for Newcomers"

This chapter explains the art of how to create open-ended events designed to attract new people. If you are just starting your singles program, "entry events" are a great way to build your attendance. If you already have a program, "entry events" open additional doors for newcomers to become involved. The information in Chapter 4 also explains the importance of keeping "entry events" as a regular part of your beginning or growing singles ministry.

### Chapter 5—"Creating Quality Events"

This chapter helps you with all the details to make sure you are offering quality events. Staging a poor quality event can often be worse than having no events at all.

## TOOLS TO HELP YOU

The resources on the following pages are designed to stimulate discussion and give examples of how to guide dream teams as they unfold. Use these—or adjust and embellish them to fit your team's situation. Remember to bathe your efforts in prayer for God's wisdom and guidance.

• **Resource 7, "Dream Team Preparation"** *(Worksheet)* Use this worksheet as a discussion and planning guide as you and those you are working with prepare for your dream team.

• **Resource 8, "Dream Team Brainstorming Session"** *(Sample Agenda)* Use this sample agenda as a guideline for the first dream team brainstorming session.

• **Resource 9, "Dream Team Result"** *(Summary Sheet)* Use this sheet to summarize and share the results of your dream team meeting with the pastor or church staff.

# DREAM TEAM PREPARATION

**Church** _____ **Date** _____

**We have completed the worksheets from Chapters 1 and 2 in *Starting a Single Adult Ministry.*** ❐ Yes ❐ No  *(If no, complete them before filling out this worksheet.)*

**1. Who will serve on our dream team?**
- Who will we intentionally invite to serve on the initial dream team for our church's single adult ministry? *(Guidelines: Have a strategic reason for inviting each person listed. Collectively, those listed should represent a broad section of singles in the congregation and community.)*

- Who has volunteered to be on this dream team?

**2. Who will facilitate the brainstorming sessions?** _____

**3. What are the proposed agenda tasks for the dream team?** *(State in your own words.)*

*(continued)*

**4. When and where will the session(s) take place?**

**5. Will we provide child care for these meetings?** ❐ Yes  ❐ No
*(If yes, who will be responsible for it?)*

Name _____  Phone _____

**6. Will we provide refreshments?** ❐ Yes  ❐ No
*(If yes, who will be responsible for them?)*

Name _____  Phone _____

**7. Will we make reading resources about single adult issues and ministry available for dream team members to scan before our first session?** ❐ Yes  ❐ No
*(If yes, list resources by title).*

**8. Has the senior pastor or a church staff member been informed about our dream team plans?** ❐ Yes  ❐ No
*(If yes, will the senior pastor attend our dream team sessions?)* ❐ Yes  ❐ No

**Comments:**

# DREAM TEAM BRAINSTORMING SESSION

## I. OPENING *(leader)*

- Open with a short prayer, such as: *Gracious God, thank You for the dream You have given us: to minister to the single adults in our church and our community. Lead us as we talk and dream about ways we can reach singles with the healing, compassionate truth brought to us through your son Jesus Christ. Amen.*
- Introduce yourself.
- Have each member introduce himself/herself and briefly tell about work, family, church involvement, or a reason he/she agreed to be a part of the team.
- Simply state the purpose of the meeting and remind the group what time the session will end.
- Distribute copies of the completed worksheets from chapters one and two to each group member, so everyone will have the facts about single adults in your community and church.

## II. GROUND RULES *(leader or brainstorming facilitator, if a different person)*

State the four "ground rules" for the brainstorming.

- Absolutely no evaluation or criticism.
- Consider any idea, no matter what the quality.
- Come up with as many ideas as possible.
- Build upon each other's ideas.

## III. BRAINSTORMING *(leader or facilitator)*

The leader or a group member should write the ideas on a flip chart or chalkboard. Someone should also record all ideas in a notebook for future reference. Following your brainstorming time, establish priorities and create a definition of your single ministry's purpose or purposes (see page 46, *Starting a Single Adult Ministry*).

## IV. CLOSING *(leader—end at the agreed-upon time)*

- Announce the date, time, and location of the next session.
- Encourage the team members to talk to at least two or three other single adults before the next session to gain input about other single adults' needs and interests to bring back to the dream team.
- State the purpose of the next meeting (to review all the comments and ideas given today, and to categorize or prioritize them for clarification of a few target areas upon which your future singles ministry should focus).
- Close with a short prayer, such as: *Almighty God, walk with us between now and our next session. Knit us together in the hope of Your vision for single adult ministry in our midst. Grant us clarity of mind and purpose as we move forward with these dreams and ideas. May Your Spirit lead us into all truth. Amen.*

# DREAM TEAM RESULTS

**Leader's Name** _____ **Date** _____

## RESULTS

**1. Names and phone numbers of people who served on the dream team:**

| Name | Phone |
|------|-------|
| _____ | _____ |
| _____ | _____ |
| _____ | _____ |
| _____ | _____ |
| _____ | _____ |
| _____ | _____ |
| _____ | _____ |
| _____ | _____ |

**2. What purpose statement did the dream team create for the proposed singles ministry?**

**3. What two to four areas of single adult ministry did the dream team target?** *(List them in order of priority.)*

*(continued)*

**4. Have you discussed the proposed singles ministry with your pastor?** ☐ Yes ☐ No
*(Summarize the feedback you received.)*

## FOLLOW-UP

**1. Contact each person who served on this initial dream team (see #1). Who would like to become part of the "leadership team" for the first event of your newly-forming singles program?** *(List the names and phone numbers of those who said yes.)*

| Name | Phone |
|------|-------|
| _____ | _____ |
| _____ | _____ |
| _____ | _____ |
| _____ | _____ |
| _____ | _____ |
| _____ | _____ |

**2. What other individuals will you invite to join the team?** *(Make sure they are—as much as is possible—from the "target" group for whom you wish to plan your first event.)*

| Name | Phone |
|------|-------|
| _____ | _____ |
| _____ | _____ |
| _____ | _____ |
| _____ | _____ |

# Points of Entry: Opening Doors for Newcomers

---

The singles ministry worker sounded frustrated as she said, "We have a problem getting our singles group to grow. The same handful of people attend every meeting and we just can't get others to come. What can we do?"

This common challenge has no "magic wand" answer. But church growth experts have discovered that ongoing "entry events" in any church or special ministry effectively attract new people. With thorough planning and strategic timing, entry events can become a regular part of your singles program. Especially if you're just getting your singles group started, entry events are a must. And the results can be exciting for everyone involved.

What is an entry event? An entry event is a church event or program specifically designed to create an open door through which new attenders may easily enter. Easy entry points are vital to beginning and maintaining a healthy, growing singles group. According to Lyle Schaller, church growth consultant at Yokefellow Institute, entry events should occur throughout every program of the church. A newcomer must be able to easily find a niche with other "first-timers," and the group identity must not have progressed so far that it seems difficult or impossible to break into the existing fellowship of long-time members.

In *Create Your Own Future!* Schaller states that churches interested in numerical growth must enhance the number, variety, and attractiveness of every "entry point" into their congregations. [1]

---

*"Most long-established churches resemble a large closed circle. . . . Most of the resources are allocated to meeting the needs of the members already within that circle. . . . If that congregation is to grow in numbers, it probably will be necessary to open several doors into that closed circle."*
—LYLE SCHALLER [2]

---

Pressure from long-time church members who want to perpetuate the status quo often hinder the development of new entry points. But without entry events to gain new members, no ministry will grow or survive.

Schaller warns that even new groups or classes in the church can unintentionally "close" very quickly as camaraderie develops. As a group meets the second, third, fourth, and more times, those who are already acquainted tend to talk most readily with each other, developing a link of friendship that squeezes out the new person. Another difficulty is that the group's leaders tend to only recruit their friends for leadership, without exploring a new person's potential for service.

This is a natural result as group identity grows stronger. But if your purpose is to reach out, your ministry must regularly create new groups or events, offering a steady diet of new places for visitors who seek a place to belong.

## THREE CORNERSTONES OF SUCCESSFUL ENTRY EVENTS

Each successful entry event is built on three basic cornerstones.

### 1. It is easy to attend.

An entry event should be scheduled on a convenient day and time for possible attenders. If single parents are involved, provide child care. Clearly publicize beginning and ending times, so those attending can plan their time accordingly. Hold the event at an easy-to-find location.

### 2. It provides a new learning experience, enrichment, or fun with others.

Few newcomers have the courage to

simply show up at a church event for no specific reason. But an "excuse" like learning how to build healthy relationships, enhance self-esteem, or resolve your kid's sibling rivalry helps people give themselves permission and a reason to step beyond the boundary of their isolation and go to an event for the first time. A purpose for coming to an event provides courage to face what may otherwise seem to be a formidable group of strangers.

**3. It creates an obvious opportunity to meet with other new people of like mind or life-style.**

It must seem to be a "new" starting point for the potential attender, where he or she will probably meet others who are also just getting started in the church, program, or group.

"We always tell everyone that newcomers are welcome, and still no one new comes!" complained a singles program participant at a regional ministry training conference. When she displayed her church's newsletter, however, it showed an advertisement for her singles game playing group which stated: "Come join us—we've been meeting every Friday night for the last three years!"

This publicity statement clearly signaled that the group had been together for some time, and was probably unintentionally "closed." So holding new entry events on a regular basis cannot be overemphasized for giving potential newcomers a continual offering of "user-friendly" starting points. It is usually a losing battle to try to channel new attenders into a group whose existing membership has been together for a long time.

The pastor in one medium-sized congregation reported he believed that a ministry to single parents was impossible, even though many single-parent families attended his church each Sunday. He had thoroughly publicized ahead of time an organizational meeting for single parents, but only two single parents showed up. He had scheduled the meeting to be an early Saturday morning breakfast held at a small restaurant several miles away from the church's neighborhood.

Was this an effective entry event? The answer is found by evaluating whether or not it was built upon the three cornerstones just described.

The first cornerstone, "easy to attend," was missing. Single parents who have their children for the weekend find Saturdays at breakfast an inconvenient time to attend a metting—especially when there is no child care available on site.

The meeting's program or agenda was not defined in the publicity—a transgression of the second cornerstone. Again, few people will negotiate the unpredictable nature of a single-parent Saturday with the children to attend a

---

## Frequency of Entry Events

**Concerning the issue of making new entry points available, how often is "on a regular basis"?** Depending on your group or the size of your program (and your purpose) you may offer entry events up to twice a month or more, or as seldom as once per quarter. A church in Wichita, Kansas, has a weekly series of fun and educational classes for adult singles called "T.N.T." (Tuesday Nights Together). These classes provide easy, weekly entry points for hundreds of people throughout south-central Kansas.

**Make sure you never hold more entry events than you can produce with excellence and quality.** Hosting a poorly-executed entry event is usually far worse than having none at all. ▶

◀ For more information about the ingredients of a quality event, see Chapter 5.

meeting where it is not clear if the investment of time will be worthwhile.

This pastor did provide the third cornerstone of creating an opportunity to meet others of like mind or life-style. But having an "organizational" meeting for new people sounds as if those who show up will leave with committee assignments, responsibilities, and perhaps long lists of phone calls to make.

What could be more threatening to a newcomer—especially to a single parent who already feels over-committed and overwhelmed while trying to juggle family and work? Organizational meetings are essential, but they are not good entry events for newcomers. The pastor in this example needed to begin with the "dream team" model described in Chapter 3 in order to get started with a single parent ministry, rather than attempting to combine initial organization with the first single-parent event.

▶ See Resource 10, "Entry Event Planner," page 68.

Historically speaking, the church offers several standard entry events through which new people join the faith community. Sunday worship service has always been the primary entry event. The church's traditional summer ice cream socials, special holiday musical performances, and even vacation Bible school can be entry points for newcomers. But most congregations are content to use these same entry events over and over, ignoring the need to design specialized entry events that attract new groups of people who are not drawn by the traditional offerings.

In a singles ministry, entry events are especially important because it is ministry with a body of people in transition. Many of the singles who are active in a program today may be gone this time next year due to relocation, marriage, job change, or other personal reasons. There is a great need in singles work to be constantly opening doors for new persons to enter.

The growing rate of newly-single people in every community renders an ever-greater potential for effective singles ministry in Christ's name—made possible by insightful planning with purpose.

One practical way to plan an entry event is to use a basic *entry event worksheet.* ◀

In Chapter 3 you found instructions on how to design an overall purpose statement to help you target ministry areas for single adults in your church and community. Now your task is to repeat the process on a smaller, more focused level to create *events* that will attract newcomers.

## SIX ESSENTIAL CRITERIA

In planning each entry event, ensure success by establishing the following essential criteria.

### 1. Who is the target group?

Who would we like to attract with this particular entry event? One thirty-year-

---

## What Brings New People to Church?

According to their nationwide surveys of "unchurched" people completed by the Barna Research Group, the most enticing reason to attend church would be a church-sponsored concert or a seminar on a topic of personal interest. The second most popular reason was if a friend invited them to attend. Nearly at the bottom of the list? If the *pastor* called or visited in the home, offering an invitation to attend.[3]

Well-targeted entry events give people a reason to begin attending church. Encouraging your members to invite their friends is essential, so make sure the events are easy for your members to bring a friend along. Relying on the pastor or staff should never be your primary means of reaching new people!

old single man, struggling to start a singles group in his church, finally put a notice in the church bulletin inviting all "singles who like to have fun and meet new people" to join him in the church parlor the following Tuesday night.

Imagine his shock when more than twenty people responded to his invitation in the bulletin—but all were retired and over sixty-five years old! The young man had been successful in drawing a crowd fitting the publicized criteria. However, the young adult singles this man had hoped for had not been clearly targeted in his advertisement.

In creating an entry point, identify who it is you want to attract to the event. Remember to be realistic! What groups of single adults did your initial dream team target for your singles ministry? Look at your congregation and neighborhood. Are most of the single people retired, young career people, or divorced with children? Make sure you've assessed accordingly and planned sensitively as you try to reach the people in mind.

### 2. What issues, needs, and interests are important to this target group?

Remember that upon the three cornerstones of a good entry event you must build the most appropriate programs for the target group. Here's a hint: the best way to find out what is important to this group is to ask them! Don't rely upon a written survey they must return via mail to you (which is almost always an exercise in futility). Personal contact and phone calling is the best way to do your homework in this area. Let some people in this target group help form your thinking and planning.

As Terry Hershey, author of *Young Adult Ministry*, suggests, the simple question, "What do you think this church should be doing or offering for _____?" works wonderfully.[4] Fill in the blank with your target group. Your

educated thinking helps ensure successful entry events.

### 3. Who will be the informal "dream team" to help design the entry event?

If you are just starting your singles ministry and have followed the suggestions in the last chapter, you will already have a group of people who have agreed to move ahead as the planning team for the first event.

If you have an existing singles program and are seeking to create new events, call a few of the people you polled for input on the target group's issues, needs, and interests. Stress that your intention is to get their perspective, ideas, and advice.

When your dream team meets, let them help you establish the event, choose a date and time, and determine the necessary ingredients for a successful event. What kinds of details might be important? For example, if the target group they represent are people with children, they'll make sure you don't forget child care, or they'll tell you the activity shouldn't run too late on a school night. If the target group they represent is older singles, they may suggest that for health reasons the refreshments should be fresh vegetable munchies rather than sweets. Their advice will be invaluable as you design your entry event with sensitivity to the target group.

### 4. What are the essentials in setting up the event?

After the dream team meeting, make a thorough list of what you will need for the entry event. ▶

One standard entry event essential is a registration table located near the front door. I should be complete with name tags and some of the friendliest people you know to greet regulars and newcomers as they arrive. A sign-in registration sheet is a good idea. A useful strategy is to place a sign beside this sheet which

◀ Refer to Resource 12, "Quality Event Evaluation," Chapter 5, page 81, for a list of things you may need for setting up an entry event.

says, "Would you like information about more events in the future? Please sign in." All of those who sign the registration sheet have given you permission to follow up with them.

---

*It's a nice touch if the senior pastor can visit or attend the entry event—even if only long enough to be introduced and to welcome the attenders. This helps newcomers become familiar with who the pastor is and indicates that this event is important enough for the pastor to attend.*

---

At the event, have everything planned completely. Look competent! Those who are new to your church will often decide whether to return by what happens at this first event they attend. Lead the entire event with a spirit of warmth, caring, professionalism, enthusiasm, and welcome.

Provide a nonthreatening way for people to meet one another through an uncomplicated ice-breaker at the beginning of each event. If your entry event features a speaker, leave ample time at the end for questions from the audience. Leave the last half hour of the event, if appropriate, for refreshments and informal socializing. Make sure the structured event ends at the publicized time—be reliable.

Most of all, remember that an entry event means no hard sell. This is not the time to demand commitment; it is a "come and see" event for new people.

Entry events are designed for a person to visit, learn more about the program, meet some new people, learn or experience something new, and have a positive church experience. An entry event is a place for you to say, "We're glad you came. Join us again anytime!" It is not the place to say, "We've tried to get new people to join our group for years. We need you. Please help us or our group will die."

Remember that people want to become part of a church or organization where they perceive things are happening. If you portray a "poor us" desperate image, you will negate the reason behind your entry event.

---

## Entry Event Examples

**What are some good examples of entry events in singles ministry?** These events work well, can be staged with a minimum effort, and appeal to a broad spectrum of people—churched and unchurched.

• *Divorce recovery workshops*

• *Single parenting seminars*

• *Speakers or forums on topics of interest* such as self-esteem, relationships, how to deal with difficult people, resolving anger, friendship, and how to discern God's will for one's life. For other current issues and themes of interest, check the self-help/personal growth shelves of both secular and Christian bookstores.

• *Social events*

• *Volleyball (or other sports)* played one night per week in the church gym or on the parking lot.

**Remember, an effective entry event at one church may not work at yours.** A "Photo Road Rally" may be a hit in rural Pennsylvania but a flop in New York City. Two excellent resources containing ideas you can tailor to your needs or use as springboards are *The Idea Catalog for Single Adult Ministry* by Jerry Jones and each issue of *Single Adult Ministries Journal.* ◄

► For more information on these resources, see the bibliography on page 190.

**5. How does this event fit into the total life of the church?**

All entry events are bridges to help bring people into the faith community where they can find support, fellowship, educational opportunities, and a life-changing encounter with Jesus Christ. You must frequently ask yourself this question as a reminder that entry events are open doors to the whole church and not just to an isolated segment of the church.

**6. How will we evaluate the event?**

Write down questions you will ask yourselves after the event is over to measure its degree of success. For example:

• *Who came? What age groups were represented? What was the ratio of men to women? Did we get the target group we expected? Why or why not?*

• *What "worked" at this event? What didn't? How will we do things differently next time?*

When you evaluate your efforts, remember not to be overcritical. The purpose of the post-event evaluation is to help your program improve overall, not to judgmentally tear it apart. Thoughtful and regular evaluation after each event helps clarify if your intentions are being enacted with a spirit of excellence. ▶

Jot down the names of people you met at the entry event who you think might like to help plan another event or serve on the next dream team. Call these few and ask them for feedback on the event. At that time, invite them to attend an informal dream team meeting to brainstorm about the next event. Most of these dream team participants soon progress into experienced leaders for ongoing planning and additional responsibilities.

Staging successful entry events is so invigorating that the vision and commitment of the singles group and the leaders cannot help but grow. From these types of contacts you will develop an ongoing leadership "core" or team who will continue to serve.

Should all those who attend an entry event receive a follow-up visit, call, or note? Don't overwhelm them. A casual note or brief phone call with the simple message, "We're glad you came. You are important to us. Please return sometime!" is more than adequate. Too much follow-up negates the relaxed "come and see" atmosphere that was created at the event. ▶

With focus and planning, your group can grow. Keep quality as your top priority as you proceed with events.

◀ Use Resource 11, "Post-Entry Event Evaluation," page 69, as a guide for evaluating each event.

◀ Need more input about the essentials of good follow-up? Chapter 6 offers advice on follow-up techniques in your singles ministry.

---

## TOOLS TO HELP YOU

On the next few pages, you will find worksheets to guide your discussions about entry event planning and evaluation. Let them help you remain targeted and intentional as you proceed.

• Use **Resource 10, "Entry Event Planner" (Worksheet)** as a discussion and planning guide as you and your team plan an entry event.

• Use **Resource 11, "Post-Entry Event Evaluation" (Worksheet)** as a discussion and evaluation guide after each entry event. For a detailed evaluation of the "nuts and bolts" (item 4), ask one or all members of the planning team to complete Resource 12, "Quality Event Evaluation," from Chapter 5.

# ENTRY EVENT PLANNER

**Proposed Event Name** _____ **Today's Date** _____

**Date of Event** _____ **Time** _____ **Place**_____

**1. Who is our "target group"?** _____

**2. What do people in this target group say are their needs, issues, and interests?**

**3. Who will be on the "dream team" for this event?** *(Fill in "Area of Responsibility" after completing number 4.)*

| Name | Phone | Area of Responsibility |
|------|-------|------------------------|
| _____ | _____ | _____ |
| _____ | _____ | _____ |
| _____ | _____ | _____ |
| _____ | _____ | _____ |
| _____ | _____ | _____ |
| _____ | _____ | _____ |

**4. What are the essentials in setting up this event?**

❏ Room _____  ❏ Child care _____

❏ Equipment _____  ❏ Advertising _____

❏ Program _____  ❏ Registration _____

❏ Refreshments _____  ❏ Other _____

**5. How is this event connected to the total life of the church? How might it help people become an integral part of this congregation?**

**6. How and when will we evaluate this event after it is held?**

**SPECIAL NOTES** *(Use the back side of this form or a separate sheet of paper.)*

# POST-ENTRY EVENT EVALUATION

**Event Name** _____

**Date** _____ **Time** _____ **Place** _____

**Target Group**_____

**1. Who were the leaders and team members responsible for this event?**

**Name**                                 **Responsibility**

_____      _____

_____      _____

_____      _____

_____      _____

_____      _____

_____      _____

_____      _____

_____      _____

**2. Did the target group attend?** ☐ Yes ☐ No
**Did others attend besides the target group?** ☐ Yes ☐ No  *(If yes, who? Briefly describe.)*

**3. Of those who attended, who should be invited to serve on the dream team for our next entry event?**

**Name**                                 **Phone**

_____      _____

_____      _____

_____      _____

_____      _____

_____      _____

_____      _____

*(continued)*

**4. What worked well and what could have been done better?** (*Registration, program, room setup, parking, child care, refreshments, activities, schedule, etc.*)

**Worked well:**                                    **Could have been done better:**

**5. Do we want to follow up on newcomers who came?** ❏ Yes ❏ No
  (*If yes, answer the following questions.*)

  • What will we do?

  • Who will do the follow-up? _____
  • When will it be completed? _____
  • To whom will a report about the follow-up be given? _____

**6. On a scale of one to ten, how would you rate this event overall?** (*Circle the number that best represents your opinion.*)

| 1 | 2 | 3 | 4 | 5 |
|---|---|---|---|---|
| poor | fair | average | good | excellent |

**7. What should we remember for the next time we hold a similar event?**

**Name of evaluator(s)** _____

# Creating Quality Events

This chapter can help you make *all* events in your single adult ministry quality ones. The suggestions here can be applied to any event—small or large, formal or informal, with or without a speaker, discussion-oriented or recovery-based.

## SET THE STAGE

### Establish high standards

If you are just starting a singles group, setting high standards for your singles ministry helps assure that a genuine sense of value will pervade the atmosphere of every activity. If you already have a singles group, rate yourselves to see how well you do in "setting the stage" for good follow-up later.

The image newcomers sense in your group is crucial. If they perceive a well-organized, positive, effective event, they will have a healthy, magnetic image of your group. ◄

### Plan frequent, effective entry points

Your singles ministry, if characterized by effective and frequent "entry points," will attract single adults from beyond your congregation. As they attend your church and your singles group, these new attenders will look for evidence that you care about them and are sensitive to their needs. You can project the genuine image of caring about those who attend your events by providing quality meetings, seminars, classes, and other ministry occasions. Newcomers will not return to a mediocre group that does not welcome them or address their needs and interests. Conduct all your programming with a spirit of excellence, down to the last detail. ". . . Do it all for the glory of God" (I Cor. 10:31). ◄

> *"Can the data be any more clear and compelling? Fewer than 1 of every 10 non-Christians stated that the Protestant church in America is very sensitive to their needs. . . . Given these perceptions, how attractive can the Church be to these nonbelievers?*
> *"The obstacle is not ignorance. Given the plethora of technologies and information resources at hand these days, what can be the excuse for not knowing and addressing the needs of the very people Jesus Himself identified as our primary ministry target?"*
> —GEORGE BARNA[1]

### Bathe efforts in prayer

Remember to include prayer as part of your preparations. Make time before every event to gather your committee or team. Together, ask God for leadership, guidance, and wisdom. After each event, share a few moments of prayerful thankfulness for the Holy Spirit's work through the ministry of your single adults. Bathing your ministry in prayer is an essential way to keep on track with what and how God is calling you to serve.

► For specific event ideas, see Chapter 4, page 66, and brainstorm with your dream team as described in previous chapters.

► For things to avoid, refer to Resource 16, "Ten Deadly Mistakes," page 88.

---

## Where Should You Meet?

**If you desire newcomers to attend your event,** try to meet at the church or at another well-known, easy-to-find location in the community. It is easier (and less anxiety-producing) to attend an event for the first time at a public location where address-hunting or parking is not a problem.

**If you are working to create bonding of a small group or team that has already formed,** meeting in someone's home helps add informality and warmth to the setting. Otherwise, hold the first few meetings or events at the church or another neutral location. Move the group's meeting place to a home setting only by the group's decision.

## USE A QUALITY EVENT CHECKLIST

The following informal "checklist" of basic elements will help you create quality events in your singles program. Add to it any other elements that are unique to your group. If you faithfully work through this checklist as you prepare for each event, you can maintain consistency in holding successful events. ▶

### 1. Meeting room or location

Make sure your meeting location is neat, clean, and well lit. Is enough seating available? Will an assigned person watch and set up more chairs if needed? Make sure extra chairs are readily accessible.

Visitors are nervous about joining strangers, and they can panic if they don't see an available chair in a convenient spot. Even if plenty of seats remain empty in the front row, set up more in the back. Make it easy for first-timers to slip in and be anonymous if they wish. Having to walk before a room of people to sit in the front is intimidating and alienating for most newcomers.

**How should the seating be arranged?** Should your chairs be in rows, or would a circle or semi-circle work better? This question is important because your seating arrangement can potentially have a dramatic impact on the success of your event.

The size of your meeting room may dictate the answer to this question. But if you do have a choice, consider these three guidelines from church growth experts:

• *If your central goal is to impart infor-mation* via a speaker, overhead projector, video, or other focalized means, place your chairs in rows (straight or gently-curved) facing the central attraction.

For example, if a police officer presents a program on "Safety Tips for Those Who Live Alone," put the chairs in fairly straight rows so the focus is on the speaker.

• *If your central goal is to focus upon group process,* place your chairs in a circle. This allows participants to see each other and makes the leader part of the circle and conversation—not above or separate from it. The best situation is to have one large circle; but if you must, add rows (as needed) in circles behind the original one.

For example, if your agenda includes a divorce support group with sharing, discussion, and prayer, circular seating would be best so that everyone will feel included and be able to see who is speaking.

• *If your goal is to impart information* and *to have group process,* place the chairs in a semi-circle, adding rows as necessary. The speaker or group leader should be in front, facing the half-circle rows. This arrangement lets the participants see each other easily, yet naturally allows focus upon the speaker or center of information.

This seating arrangement is useful for an event like a single parents' class. The speaker might provide information and ideas about parental issues, followed by questions from the participants and general group discussion. Seating at round tables also works well for a gathering with

◀Resource 12, "Quality Event Evaluation," page 81, can help you plan effective events. Its use is described in "Tools to Help You," page 80.

---

## Minimize the Number One Social Fear

According to a study reported in the *Single Adult Ministries Journal,*[2] the number one social fear is entering a roomful of strangers. In fact, most people would rather speak in public (social fear number two) than walk into a gathering of people they don't know. Therefore, your leadership team should plan accordingly to minimize the "fear factor" guests may feel when entering your singles group for the first time.

this dual goal. Tables also allow the participants to manage refreshments or have a surface to take notes on at the same time.

*Is your meeting place easy to find?* Publicity should meet the following criteria to make it easy for people to get to the event.

• *Give clear directions to your location.*

• *Indicate where to park a car (if parking is a challenge).*

• *Tell which door is the right one to enter.* (Churches are especially notorious for having many entrances.)

In order to attend your event, newcomers need to know how to get to its location! This information should be clearly stated in your publicity pieces. ◄

New people usually have no idea where to find "the parlor" or "fellowship hall." Hang large signs on every entrance door of the building with directions to the correct entrance door or meeting room. If it's an evening or weekend event, make sure the church doors are unlocked! This small detail is frequently overlooked—but visitors won't wait around long for someone to come to the rescue before they leave and find something else to do with their time.

Some newly-single adults struggle with having the courage to accept their new identity; they often find it immensely diffi-

cult to attend a singles event for the first time. (Singles ministry workers routinely receive phone calls from potential visitors who came to the church for a singles activity, only to drive back home because they didn't have the courage to walk through the front door.) To ease their uncertainty, station a greeter inside the main entrance to welcome people and point them in the right direction. Also station greeters outside the building by the main entrance to offer visitors a friendly face and clear reassurance that they have come to the right place.

## 2. Greeters—the first people newcomers meet

Don't choose just anyone to be greeters at your singles event. The greeters at the entrances to your building and meeting room are "image setters." These people give visitors a first impression of your group and may immediately impact their feelings about being there. To help visitors be glad they came, invite the most relaxed, friendly, quality people you know to be greeters.

*Qualifications.* Ideally, greeters should have the following qualities:

• *Have the gift of hospitality and genuinely enjoy people.*

• *Have the "right" degree of friendliness* (don't smother newcomers).

▶ Quality publicity is a powerful tool for creating a positive image of your ministry. Chapter 10 tells how to successfully promote and publicize your singles events.

---

### Respect Visitors' Personal Space

**A fine line distinguishes the amount of attention that is appropriate for greeters to give.** In *User-Friendly Churches,* George Barna points out that the church has always tried to make sure visitors are never anonymous. Traditional thinking has stressed that the more attention given to a visitor, the better-welcomed that person will feel. Research reveals, however, that the opposite is true. Too much recognition and attention makes visitors feel their "personal space" has been trespassed and that unwelcome pressure has been heaped upon them.[3]

**Allow visitors to be cautious and anonymous.** Newcomers want to "check out" your program and decide if it offers what they are looking for. Do not insist that all visitors stand or be introduced to the entire group. Simply greet each person with a friendly smile and "We're glad you came!" This relieves the pressure that often makes visitors feel alienated, freeing them to be no more than observer, if they wish.

- *Have the ability to create the impression that your singles group as a "safe place" for the first-time visitor.*

- *Have the ability to comfortably move the newcomer from the entrance into the group.*

**Responsibilities.** Greeters should be in place at least fifteen minutes before the event begins. At least two or more greeters should be stationed at the following places:

- *At all entrances to the building through which attenders can enter.*

- *At the registration table, inviting people to sign in and make name tags, giving them informational materials about your singles ministry and church.*

- *"Floating" in the meeting room, making sure visitors find seats near others and are introduced to at least one or two regular attenders.*

- *In the parking lot, for events which attract many first-time persons to your church.*

**Tips for greeters.** Greeters should not be people who are "checking out" new arrivals for potential dating prospects. They should be individuals who are genuinely interested in people and can offer a warm smile and relaxed manner. While meeting people socially is certainly an important aspect of single life, aggressive "come-ons" are a negative factor to first-time visitors—and are *especially* hard to tolerate if imposed by greeters!

One other note about this: your greeters may need to try to steer new attenders away from the handful in your group whose demeanor is too aggressive. Nearly every singles ministry has a few people who attend only to meet potential dates and to get their phone numbers as quickly as possible. Your singles group may soon gain the reputation of seeming like a "meet market" or a dating service unless your greeters consistently model otherwise.

**Enlisting everyone as "greeters."** Your event will feel warm and welcoming if you can create an atmosphere in which it is clear that *everyone* is a host. You can help instill this attitude through these ideas:

- *Have the leader of the event, in the welcoming comments, simply state, "Everyone is a host or hostess here. Let's make each other feel welcome!"*

- *At the beginning of the event, ask everyone to stand, find two or three people they have never met, and introduce themselves.*

- *If fewer than twenty-five people are present, briefly go around the room and let everyone share his or her name and one non-threatening personal fact.*

Brainstorm ahead of time with your leadership team about other ways to create a friendly, open atmosphere at your events without invading the privacy of the first-time visitors or demanding they reveal too much about themselves. Hospitality is critical.

## Parking Lot Greeters

**Many churches have a team of "parking lot greeters" on Sundays or for weeknight events. At Frazier Memorial United Methodist Church in Montgomery, Alabama, such volunteers direct cars to parking spaces and greet people as they arrive. According to senior minister John Ed Mathison, "It makes a good impression on a visitor to have a parking lot usher offer assistance—giving directions, helping with small children, sheltering under an umbrella, and in many other ways. It is important for this (often) first impression to be a positive, friendly one."[4] Especially for single adults, feeling welcome and comfortable are two essentials at any event. How is your church and singles group doing with your "welcome" efforts?**

During the event itself, your group must continue to foster the "friendliness quotient." You may decide to employ an additional icebreaker (also called a "crowdbreaker") or other means through which everyone has a chance to interact. Make sure everyone shakes hands, speaks to at least a few people, and is spoken to by others. Try not to let anyone remain isolated.

### 3. The actual event ◄

*Whatever you do, make sure it's quality!* Be honest in your publicity or promotional materials about what you will provide, then provide what you have promised. New people are dissatisfied when an event appears disorganized, ill-prepared, and poorly executed.

*Respect the time frame you have advertised.* Begin and end the event at the times you publicized. Do not wait for stragglers before starting. If you do, you are saying to those who arrived on time that they aren't important enough for you to start. By beginning and ending promptly, you communicate that you know time is important. Your attenders will learn they can count on your program to deliver (schedule-wise) what it has promised. The child care workers also depend on you to begin and end promptly.

One visitor to a church singles group reported the following example of the importance of honoring those who arrive

on time. This adult showed up punctually for a 7:30 p.m. event as a first-time visitor. Only the group leader and a few other newcomers were present when he came. Fifteen minutes later, several regular attenders arrived.

"Have you started yet?" they asked the leader. "No," he answered, "no one was here yet, so I decided to wait."

"No one" to the leader probably meant "none of the regular attenders." But to the newcomers who had arrived on time and were kept waiting, "no one" meant they did not count. This single adult did not return to the singles group because he did not receive the message that his presence and time were valuable.

*Keep announcements brief and to the point.* Nearly every group gathering will call for some general announcements. A good rule of thumb is to make only the announcements that are absolutely necessary. For further announcements about coming events, prepare flyers that people can pick up as they arrive or leave.

The announcer does not have to be the head of the leadership team. More importantly, he or she needs to be the person among you who is the most natural and comfortable before groups and can be trusted to follow the leadership's agenda.

Beforehand, write down the comments that should be made to introduce the event, and make sure the announcer

► For some general guidelines on how to hold effective meetings, see Tool 1, page 184, in the Appendix.

---

## What about Name Tags?

**Never insist that a newcomer wear a name tag if he or she is reluctant. However, wearing name tags at your church events is advantageous to everyone. It helps the leadership team begin to recognize and remember names of attenders; it helps visitors know who is sitting nearby; and it helps create the "everyone's a host" atmosphere.**

**"Only 9 percent of plateaued churches and 2 percent of declining churches used name tags in Sunday school, as compared to a full 28 percent of larger growing churches," reports C. Kirk Hadaway in *Church Growth Principles* .[5] Smaller churches, on the other hand, tend not to use name tags because they feel it implies that the church is no longer a "family." Yet first-time visitors in the small church often feel excluded because of this strong "family" feel.**

sticks to them. Extemporaneous comments that are unrelated, inappropriate, or "insider" jokes will immediately alienate newcomers. Have two or three people work together preparing the introductions and announcements to insure quality control. ▶

If your planning team would like an opening prayer during the announcement time, check to make sure the announcer feels comfortable praying in public. If not, you may ask another person to offer the opening prayer or write out a brief prayer for the announcer to read.

At each event, briefly reiterate your singles ministry "purpose statement" during the announcements. (See Chapter 3 on how to create a purpose statement.) This reminder helps keep the group's focus on the central aim of your singles ministry. It also familiarizes the new attenders with your group's general principles.

*Use an icebreaker/crowdbreaker.* To help people relax and get acquainted, use an icebreaker or crowdbreaker—an activity that helps people interact and share something fun or non-threatening about themselves.

*Satisfy needs and interests with good content (speaker/discussion/etc.)* To accomplish this goal, it is critical that you and your planning team plan well in advance of the event and weigh each idea against the needs and interests of your group. ▶

*Serve refreshments—good food is a grand essential!* Like icebreakers,

◀ See Resource 13, "Welcome and Announcements," page 83.

◀ Use the questions on Resource 14, "Topic, Program, and Speaker Ideas— Are They Relevant?" page 85, to make sure the main content of each event scratches where people itch.

---

## Announcement Dos and Don'ts

Some statements should *not* be made during announcement time at your events. Following is a list of such statements (actually heard at singles' functions) and why you should not say them. Note the corresponding list of things that should be said instead.

| DO NOT SAY | DO SAY |
|---|---|
| **1. "Not many people showed up tonight, but I guess we'll go ahead."** This communicates to people that they are almost not valuable enough to make it worth having the event. Always proceed with your event, even if only a few people come. Success is not measured in numbers. God's Spirit may have prompted those few people to attend for an important purpose. | **1. "We are delighted you have come!"** If you must comment on the size of the meeting, simply say, "Just the right size of group is here to benefit from this program." |
| **2. "Please, please come back again. We need new people in our group, because we've lost a lot of members."** No one wants to be part of a dying group! | **2. "We're glad you came. We think our singles group is an exciting and growing place, and we're glad you decided to be a part of what's happening tonight."** |
| **3. "The single life is really tough. We singles (or divorced people) need to stick together."** Such a comment creates a negative image of singleness and goes against one of the redemptive purposes of your singles group—to help people learn to appreciate the positive aspects of being single. | **3. "We are a gathering of single adults who are looking for ways to grow spiritually, emotionally, mentally, and socially. We hope you will find ways to grow into your fullest potential by being a part of our group."** |

refreshments can help people relax and get acquainted informally.

Secure volunteers who will arrive early to make sure you have enough cups, napkins, plates, and other supplies on hand. Are the coffee pots clean? Are the refreshments arranged in an appealing, sanitary manner?

Remember some people are on sugar- or salt-restricted diets. Offer appropriate alternatives that are fresh and low in sugar and salt content, alongside the traditional cookies whenever possible. It's simplest to serve refreshments that are convenient to eat; if they're messy, provide plates and tableware. Always have at least one non-caloric, decaffeinated beverage choice available, even if it's just ice water (add lemon slices for a refreshing touch).

Who provides the refreshments? Every singles ministry discovers its own unique way of supplying them. Some options include:

• *Recruit volunteers to bring them.*

• *Purchase refreshments and ask for a donation from each person to cover expenses* (or place a bowl on the refreshment table for donations).

• *Have a few people meet and make the refreshments together ahead of time or even the day before.* Baking cookies together can be great fun and offers an opportunity to build relationships.

Asking people individually to bring refreshments usually works better than passing a sign-up sheet. And, unless your church will provide you the tableware, cups, and napkins, you can handle these items the same way.

Cancel refreshments if no one wants to bring them. Having coffee, iced tea, or ice water alone works just fine, if necessary.

### 4. Child care—your most important asset

A major comfort-level indicator for single parents attending your events is the child care your church offers. If you hope to attract single adults whose children are not too young to stay home alone, offering child care is a must.

***Staffing.*** Child care greatly enhances single parents' ability to attend your events; but don't offer it unless you can do so safely and with quality. Single parents find it hard to concentrate or enjoy an event if they think your child-care staff may not be qualified or competent to care for their children.

Check with your church office to find out if child care guidelines have been established by your congregation. Your church may also have a list of volunteers or people for hire, who can staff your event's child care room. Don't wait until the last minute to enlist child care workers! Staffing the child care should be one of the first items accomplished when preparing for an event. Always have two people present in each child care room.

Possible child care workers include:

• *High school teens from the youth program.*

• *Older (or retired) adults in your congregation.*

---

## Child Care—Make It Sparkle!

According to *Church Planter,* when people visit your church their most lasting impression usually doesn't come from the applicability of the sermon or the hospitality of the congregation. It's the nursery! Therefore, make it a top priority to keep the nursery (or child care) area functional and appealing.

The child care area should be clean and well-lit. Broken toys and worn-out books should be replaced. The entire room, toys, sheets, cribs, and changing tables should be sanitized regularly. Neither sick children nor sick workers should be allowed. —Robert Lee[6]

• *A married couple who support the singles ministry.*

• *Volunteers from within the singles ministry who are not involved in the event.*

• *Members of the children's ministry department at your church.*

• *Outside people who are professional child care providers.*

Offer child care only for the ages your sitters can safely and competently manage. A single parent will not return to your church if his or her children are injured or neglected in your child care room.

**Procedures and activities.** When parents arrive, have them put name tags with first and last names on their children. Invite them to complete a brief "parent's form" for the child care workers, so the parent can be found quickly in case of an emergency. ▶

If you ask parents to complete a form each time they leave children, it reminds them that you are trying to provide quality, safe care and that you need their cooperation.

If possible, instruct child care providers to do more than simply "herd the masses." Make sure the ingredients for simple, constructive activities and games are available to the child care workers. Have someone on the leadership team periodically check on the child care room during every event. This will ensure quality control while letting the child care workers know you support and appreciate them.

One singles ministry has developed a specific child care program for the children of parents attending the singles events. A volunteer "coordinator" checks the singles ministry calendar a month ahead and notes when (and for how long) child care will be needed. The coordinator meets monthly with an advisory committee of single adults invited to serve because they work professionally in jobs involving children: preschool and elementary teachers, as well as a manager of a commercial child care, plus a single adult who works as the children's program director at a local YMCA. Together they plan simple, interesting activities for toddlers or preschool children and activities for kindergarten children through third grade. They list supplies needed and design a basic "schedule" for each child care period that month, much like a simple lesson plan.

The coordinator is responsible to make sure the needed supplies are on hand and gives a copy of the basic schedule and activity instructions to the child care workers prior to each occasion. The results include meaningful and fun opportunities for the children, satisfaction for single parents, and the sense of a job well done for the child care workers (who appreciate ideas and a sense of structure).

Your child-care policies and format may evolve as your ministry changes. Review the child care procedures and activities regularly and update as necessary.

NOTE: Emphasize that child-care service is only provided for single parents to use while they are actually present in the church. Federal and state laws stipulate specific regulations about child care if parents leave the premises. It may be illegal for your church to provide child care without a permit if the parent leaves the building.

◀ See Resource 15, "Singles Ministry Child Care—Parent's Form," page 86.

## RATE YOUR EVENTS

The leaders of one struggling singles ministry explained they had difficulties attracting healthy, sharp single adults to events. The few newcomers who did attend did not return. When the members of the leadership team were asked to rate the quality of their singles program on a scale of one to ten, each member rated their events at either five or six.

In the discussion that followed, they

admitted they didn't invite quality friends to the singles program because they did not believe their events were high-quality. The leadership team discovered that without making a concerted effort to create top-notch events, they would not interest or attract first-class single adults. Staging quality events does not require a large budget, but it does require planning and attention to detail.

Based on the principles in this chapter, how do you rate your singles events?

## TOOLS TO HELP YOU

Strive to develop quality events with a spirit of excellence. Use the worksheets on the following pages to help you cover all the bases.

• **Resource 12, "Quality Event Evaluation"** *(Survey Form)* The leadership team should use this reproducible resource as a guideline for setting up a successful event. After each event, have a different team member (or an event participant) fill out another copy to measure your success with your standards. Keep these completed "before-and-after" checklists on file to help document your improvement and remind you of changes you want to make the next time you hold a similar gathering.

• **Resource 13, "Welcome & Announcements"** *(Sample Outline)* Follow this suggested outline for your welcome and announcements. Use it to keep on track with relaying important information at meetings in a brief, open, friendly manner.

• **Resource 14, "Topic, Program, and Speaker Ideas—Are They Relevent?"** *(Evaluation Guide)* The four questions on this resource sheet make it easy for you and your planning team to evaluate the relevency of each topic, program, or speaker idea.

• **Resource 15, "Singles Ministry Child Care—Parent's Form"** *(Sample)* Use this sample form as a pattern for making up your own. If you want the form to protect you legally (and that's always a good idea), have your church's legal advisor revise it accordingly.

• **Resource 16, "Ten Deadly Mistakes"** *(Discussion Guide)* Are your events set up and conducted so that visitors will want to come back? Use this discussion guide occasionally with your planning team. It can help you stay on track and avoid the common but deadly errors that lower the quality of your ministry.

# QUALITY EVENT EVALUATION

Event_____ Date_____

Rate each of the following on a 1-5 scale with 1 being poor and 5 being excellent.

## 1. Meeting Room or Location                 poor          excellent

| | |
|---|---|
| Clean and well-lit? | 1 2 3 4 5 |
| Comfortable temperature? | 1 2 3 4 5 |
| Adequate number of chairs and tables? | 1 2 3 4 5 |
| Easy to find? | 1 2 3 4 5 |
| Directions to location clearly described in publicity? | 1 2 3 4 5 |
| Enough parking? | 1 2 3 4 5 |
| Location clearly marked with signs? | 1 2 3 4 5 |

## 2. Greeters

| | |
|---|---|
| Adequate number? | 1 2 3 4 5 |
| Arrived early? | 1 2 3 4 5 |
| Sufficient instructions/training on how to be a greeter? | 1 2 3 4 5 |
| Placed at strategic places to meet visitors? | 1 2 3 4 5 |
| Registration table present? | 1 2 3 4 5 |
| Name tags and pens available? | 1 2 3 4 5 |
| Literature about the singles programs/church available? | 1 2 3 4 5 |
| Newcomers not embarrassed by too much attention? | 1 2 3 4 5 |

## 3. Actual Event

| | |
|---|---|
| Provided what was promised in the publicity? | 1 2 3 4 5 |
| Began on time? | 1 2 3 4 5 |
| Ended on time? | 1 2 3 4 5 |
| Announcements—clear, inclusive, brief? | |
| Icebreaker/crowdbreaker included? | 1 2 3 4 5 |
| Content (speaker/topic/etc.) interesting and relevant? | 1 2 3 4 5 |
| Group interaction/activities dynamic? | 1 2 3 4 5 |
| All program needs (projector/handouts/etc.) set up ahead? | 1 2 3 4 5 |
| Refreshments—good quality, plentiful, and appropriate? | 1 2 3 4 5 |

*(continued)*

| | poor | excellent |
|---|---|---|
| **4. Child Care**<br>Child care offered safely and sufficiently? | | 1 2 3 4 5 |
| **5. Other** _____ | | 1 2 3 4 5 |
| **Your overall rating of this event:** | | **1 2 3 4 5** |

**Comments:**

**What could be done to improve this event in the future?**

**Name** _____ **Phone** _____

# WELCOME AND ANNOUNCEMENTS

**Event** _____ **Date** _____ **Time** _____

**Location** _____

**Chairperson** _____ **Announcer** _____

Announcements should be prepared and/or reviewed by at least two people. Duplicate this resource and use it as an outline for developing a welcome and announcements for each event you hold.

**1. WELCOME:** "Welcome to _____ Church and our singles program. My name is _____. We are glad you decided to be a part of our singles community for this event. If you are here for the first time, let us know how we can help you feel at home and make your experience both enjoyable and beneficial."

**2. OPENING PRAYER (optional):** "Please bow your heads for a moment of prayer."
*(Write out prayer here, if helpful.)*

**3. ICEBREAKER/INTRODUCTIONS:** "Let's take a few minutes to get acquainted."
*(List the brief "icebreaker" or introduction you will use.)*

**4. PURPOSE:** "The purpose of our singles ministry is . . ."

*(continued)*

**5. IMPORTANT FACTS:** "If you have not been in our church building before, here are a few facts you should know.

- The rest rooms are located _____.
- The drinking fountains are located _____.
- The child care room is located _____
  _____and will close at _____A.M./P.M.
- Refreshments will be available __*(before/during/after)*__ the event.
- Optional: We will be taking a break at _____A.M./P.M."
- Other facts: _____
  _____
  _____
  _____

**6. ANNOUNCEMENTS:** "Upcoming events in our singles ministry (and in our church in general) which may be of interest to you are:

_____
_____
_____
_____
_____."

*(Make announcements as brief as possible. If you can, provide flyers with full details for participants. Do not spend time on specific details of future events if you have written material available with the same information.)*

**7. INTRODUCTION:** "Our event today is _____.
It will be led/presented by _____."
Other introductory comments about the program: "_____
_____
_____
_____
_____
_____."

**Announcements for this event were prepared and/or reviewed by:**

Name _____

Name _____

# TOPIC, PROGRAM, AND SPEAKER IDEAS —ARE THEY RELEVANT?

Even though you may have created effective publicity, adequate room setup, friendly greeters, and all the other components comprising the framework for your event, the content of your event is crucial. All the "window dressing" in the world will not compensate for a program that does not offer interest and relevancy to the single adult life—and, more importantly, singles will not attend at all if the advertised topic or theme does not appeal.

Here are some questions to ask as you choose topics, programs, or speakers for your singles ministry events. If you cannot answer yes to any of these questions, you may want to reevaluate your ideas.

1. **Does this topic/program/speaker offer the attender information that will contribute to personal growth?** By attending, will people learn how to live a better life, feel more comfortable with who they are, feel more secure about their spiritual growth, feel more competent in their relationship skills, or feel more confident about the future? Is there something about the topic/program/speaker which will "grab" potential attenders and convince them that they want or need to gain this information? For example, a speaker on "self-esteem" may attract more widespread interest than a professor who shows slides of an archeological dig. While both are important, it makes sense to chose topics and programs that are of broad general appeal and save the specialized topics for small interest groups.

2. **Does this topic/program/speaker offer fun entertainment that appeals to the target audience?** It's important that some of your events be social or entertainment-oriented, though keeping a good balance of all types of events is important. For example, would your singles group enjoy a contemporary Christian vocalist providing a musical concert, or would a more traditional hymn-sing have more appeal?

3. **Does this topic/program/speaker offer social interaction opportunities for the participants?** Even though you may have brought in the best speaker available, participants may question the value of the event if they have no opportunity for conversation and meeting new people. Build interaction into every event you hold. Encourage your guest speakers to include interactive components in their presentations.

4. **Does this topic/program/speaker offer a distinctive Christian emphasis?** While heavy-duty evangelism is not appropriate for all your events, neither should you leave out the opportunity to have the "distinctively different" perspective or atmosphere that only the ministry of Christ can provide. At an "entry event," you may want to provide the Christian emphasis in a more subtle manner, since unchurched people will be trying your program for the first time. But at a singles leadership retreat, you may choose to have "faith-meets-life" topics of the Christian faith on the program agenda.

Not all events will offer both interesting information and entertainment, but all should include the Christian emphasis. Keep these guidelines as your criteria as you plan the events for your singles ministry.

# SINGLES MINISTRY CHILD CARE —PARENT'S FORM

Please complete this form and leave it with our child care providers. Together we can make sure your child is safe while at our church.

**Parent's name** _____

**Address** _____ **ZIP**_____

**Home phone** _____

**In case of emergency,** where can we find you in our church building?

Name of event _____

Room location_____

**Children's arrival time** in child care:_____

**Children's pickup time** from child care: _____

    Will you pick up your child(ren)? ❑ yes ❑ no

    If no, who will?

    Name_____

**Please complete for the children you have in child care for this event:**

| Child's name | Age | Grade | Special instructions for child's care and/or supplies brought to be picked up with child (bottles, diaper bags, toys, etc.) |
|---|---|---|---|
| 1. _____ | _____ | _____ | _____ |
| | | | _____ |
| | | | _____ |
| | | | _____ |
| 2. _____ | _____ | _____ | _____ |
| | | | _____ |
| | | | _____ |
| | | | _____ |

*(continued)*

| Child's Name | Age | Grade | Special instructions for child's care and/or supplies brought to be picked up with child (bottles, diaper bags, toys, etc.) |
|---|---|---|---|
| 3. _____ | ____ | ____ | _____ |
| | | | _____ |
| | | | _____ |
| | | | _____ |
| 4. _____ | ____ | ____ | _____ |
| | | | _____ |
| | | | _____ |
| | | | _____ |

**Other notes:**

Before signing this form, please make a name tag for each of your children who will be staying in our child care area.

**Signature** _____ **Date** _____

# TEN DEADLY MISTAKES

**The following ten deadly mistakes guarantee that visitors won't return:**

1. **Overwhelm newcomers with attention.**
   According to Barna, visitors like the option of remaining anonymous if they wish, allowing them to attend without fanfare or immediate commitment.

2. **Don't start the event on time.**
   Disorganization or tardiness signals visitors that you are careless and unprepared.

3. **Have poor (or no) greeters at the door.**
   Greeters convey the initial impression newcomers will have of your group.

4. **Let the "emcee" have free rein with his/her announcements and commentary.** If the emcee does not prepare the announcements together with your leadership team, you run the risk of projecting less than a positive image of your group, excluding newcomers with "insider" joking or omitting important welcoming and informative statements that should be made.

5. **Allow your program or event not to deliver what was advertised.**
   Being true to your publicity is essential to quality programming.

6. **Omit time for newcomers to connect with others or to get more information.** If visitors leave without having met anyone else, or without additional details about your singles ministry or church, they will not believe the time spent has been worthwhile.

7. **"Huddle" together as a leadership team during the entire event, ignoring the attenders and visitors.** The most effective leadership of your ministry will be those who understand how to reach out to others.

8. **Don't end on time.**
   Visitors will not believe you respect their schedule if the activity they have attended lasts far longer than they had planned.

9. **Let the child care be poor quality.**
   Single-parent visitors need to know their children are safe and well cared for while they are at your events.

10. **Be overly aggressive in visitor follow-up.**
    One postcard or brief phone call is adequate to thank a newcomer for attending.

# All about Follow-Up

In church ministry, *follow-up* is how and what you do to encourage people who have attended your church programs to return. Should you send a letter? Make a phone call? Visit them in person?

## WHAT DETERMINES EFFECTIVE FOLLOW-UP?

How to do effective follow-up is an art in itself. And, paradoxically, it must begin before the first person ever shows up at a church activity. How you plan and carry out an entry event largely determines whether follow-up with new people who attended will be productive. If you have set the stage for good follow-up by presenting a quality event, many newcomers will be ready and willing to return.

At one church, the ministry's attendance more than tripled in five years. Yet little or no formal follow-up contact was ever organized. Why the growth without traditional forms of follow-up? The single adult leaders created events with a spirit of true excellence. As a result, participants were eager to return. While some sort of follow-up for newcomers is important as a rule, this example illustrates what great "drawing power" quality events alone can have.

Always remember that "image" is a critical factor in promoting and building your singles group or program (see Chapter 2). If your program is perceived as filled with bright, capable, creative adults on a healthy life-style track, you will have a positive image which will impact newcomers. If, however, first-time visitors sense an attitude of poor, lonely singles who struggle with the handicap of not being married, no amount of contact will convince them to return. An image problem almost always guarantees follow-up difficulties.

If your activity has been successful and your participants feel they have experienced a worthwhile event, your follow-up efforts will be like announcing an encore after a standing ovation. First-time visitors will already be feeling positive about your singles program. Follow-up offered soon after the event can have a significant impact when the right stage has thus been set.

*The definition of "follow-up" is important to clarify.* Good follow-up is not coercion, persuasion, or attempts to convince. It is a warm invitation to return and become involved. Before you decide which methods of follow-up to use, create a definition about what your follow-up should accomplish and in what spirit it should be done. Then proceed with plans to accomplish your definition.

---

## What Helps Newcomers Come Back!

A newcomer is likely to come back to your singles ministry if he or she has had a positive experience at an entry event. That positive experience might be expressed in statements such as these:

- "I felt welcomed and 'safe.' No one pressured me to disclose any more about myself than I wished to reveal."
- "I felt informed. I received clear information about the event, the group, and its purpose."
- "I had an educational, entertaining, or enjoyable experience."
- "I met at least one other person with whom I can feel comfortable at the next event."
- "I realize that this singles ministry has something to offer that is worth gaining (friendships, spiritual growth, educational, or social opportunities, for example)."

## What Are Some Follow-Up Methods?

### 1. Newcomer registration sign-in

Placing a sign-in registration sheet at each event is one way to gain the first-timer's permission for further contact. You may want to make signing in optional, but write on a placard next to the sign-in sheet: "To receive additional information about our singles program, please sign in."

Those who sign their name, address, and phone number have given you the "green light" to contact them. If you pursue the option of home visits, you could have a place on the registration form labeled, "Would you like a home visit from our singles ministry?" Those who would like a visit could check a box.

This method can also help you build a mailing list for your singles group.

Carefully guard the names, addresses, and phone numbers you gain through registration sheets. Those on the list have given their personal information for church records only, not for loaning to other groups or for personal use. Protect the privacy of those who trust you with this information. ▶

### 2. Postcards and letters

Mailing visitors a note or postcard after the event is a friendly, non-threatening way to tell them you were glad they came. It can also communicate that you welcome them to join your group again anytime. Your leadership team will want to decide who should sign the letter or card. Options include the senior minister or staff person, your leadership team, the team's chairperson, or one of the greeters.

A two-sentence, handwritten note or postcard makes a better impression than a form letter. Taking the time to hand-write messages personalizes mail contact.

Make sure your message is general and cannot be misconstrued. An unfortu-nate example of mail follow-up happened after a divorce support-group meeting. A leadership team member wrote a post-card with this message to each person in the support group:

*"Dear____, It was good to be with you last Saturday night. I look forward to seeing you again this week. —Jane."*

Jane sent one of her postcards to a newly-separated man in a tiny town. When her postcard reached the small-town local post office, the postmaster read the message. By noon, the man who had attended the event received phone calls from several people, including his estranged wife, who wanted to know more about this "other woman." That small community speculated for weeks about the woman who wrote the card, while the man protested his innocence. Needlesstosay, when he returned to the divorce support group the next week, the man requested that he not receive any more postcards!

Following is an example of an appro-priate, safe message that could be placed on a post card:

*Dear _____,*
*We're glad you attended (name of event) a few days ago. Please join us again anytime! If we can help you with more information about our church or our singles ministry, don't hesitate to call the church office at _____.*
*Sincerely,*
*(Name)*
*_____ Church's Singles Ministry*

A longer message for a letter might read like this:

*Dear _____,*
*We're glad you attended (name of event) a few days ago. Our single adult ministry is designed to help people grow*

◀ Photocopy Resource 17, "Registration Sign-In Sheet," page 95, for use at your events.

*spiritually, emotionally, and socially. With the support of our entire congregation, our singles group fulfills these goals through a variety of activities and learning opportunities. If you're looking for a place to explore your relationship to God, to yourself, and to others, this may be the place for you!*

*If we can help you with more information about our church or our singles ministry, call us at (church phone number). We welcome you anytime!*

   *Sincerely,*

   *(Name)*

_____*Church's Singles Ministry*

If you are writing notes, you may want to include personal comments about the meaningfulness of the singles ministry to you. For example:

• "I became involved in our singles group a few months ago. Since then I have found a new purpose for living, as well as great friendships."

• "I looked around for a church home extensively before I became a part of this one. It's a great place for single adults."

### 3. Phone Calls

A phone call can be an effective means of touching base with a newcomer, but be sensitive and intentional if you choose this method of follow-up. Make your phone call short, to the point, and friendly. Have a reason for the call. People are busy, and do not welcome anything resembling a "sales" call. Remember that the quality of the event they have already attended will have spoken for itself. ◄

Your job is to thank them for coming, invite them to attend again, and answer any questions. A typical follow-up phone call should take about two minutes. Some singles ministries have females call females and males call males to avoid any mixed messages or misconstruing of purpose.

Do not make repeated follow-up phone calls to the same individuals. One call is

► Do you need some guidelines for follow-up phone calls? See Resource 18, "What to Say on the Phone," page 96.

adequate. Carefully record which visitors receive a follow-up contact. If you make a second call to the visitor, have a very good reason for doing so. Otherwise, you will become an annoying representative of your singles program.

Occasionally your phone follow-up team may call someone who is lonely, needy, or hurting. The caller should be kind, caring, and receptive to listening because ministry happens in such moments. But staying on the phone for an hour or two in a follow-up call is usually beyond the scope of suitability.

How should this kind of situation be handled? The caller could appropriately refer the person to one of the ministry's support groups or to the church's pastor for counseling or referral. The follow-up team members should never be expected to act as impromptu counselors. Nor should a phone volunteer use the opportunity to invite people for dates. Stick to the purpose of the call.

Answering machines are now a "way of life" in the world of singleness. Some people are frequently away from home; others screen their calls. When your calling team reaches an answering machine, leave a concise message, stating your reason for calling. You do not need to ask them to return your call, but you may wish to leave the church's phone number in case they want more information. Always state your name and that you are calling on behalf of your church's singles program.

If you leave a message on a first-time visitor's answering machine, consider your phone follow-up complete. Do not keep calling in an attempt to catch the visitor at home.

### 4. Home visits

Traditionally, churches have always used personal visitation as a method to follow-up visitors. The "home visit" is still used by pastors for bereavement or shut-in calls. In some churches it is still an accepted way to check on a visitor's interest level.

However, depending on your local context, this is probably not the recommended method for following up on visitors to your singles ministry events. Busy work and activity schedules make private, uninterrupted "at-home time" a precious commodity. Your unannounced house call may be met with displeasure or hostility. In many parts of our country, people don't trust strangers (even those who claim to be pastors) who wish to visit in their homes, and may even be alienated by the suggestion.

If you feel you have reasons to make home visits, first check with your pastor for support and advice about outlining a home visit follow-up program for your singles ministry. If you decide on this method, these guidelines are recommended:

• *Always call ahead and set up an appointment to stop by. Do not arrive unannounced.* On the phone, tell the person how long your visit will be, so he or she will know what to expect.

• *Have clear purposes in mind for your visit* (to thank the person for coming to your singles event, to extend an invitation to return, and to see if the person has any questions about your group).

Do not stay longer than stated in your initial phone call.

• *Take along literature from your church (flyers, newsletters, and information sheets) about your singles ministry and about the church in general.*

• *Make your visit with a partner.* If you, your calling partner, and the visitor receiving the call are the same sex, it again prevents misunderstandings of purpose.

Keep in mind that for most single adults, a home visit would probably not be appropriate after simply attending an "entry event" (a "come and see" event with low commitment and easy anonymity). Singles like to check things out before they make a commitment. A home visit to a first-timer in the singles program may come on too strong. Unless a first-timer requests a home visit, this may not be the best route of follow-up.

## WHO SHOULD DO THE FOLLOW-UP?

Your leadership team must decide this. Research with single adults across America revealed that, when asked what would make them more interested in attending a church, the least favorable response was receiving a telephone call or a personal visit from the church's minister.[1] This is a fascinating insight, considering that the typical church has tradi-

---

### Does Your Follow-Up Overwhelm Newcomers?

**Is it possible to overwhelm a visitor with follow-up?** According to one single adult, the answer is a resounding yes. "It became a game for me to watch what lengths various churches would go to in order to 'win' me to their congregation," she relates. "After my first visit, one church brought me cinnamon rolls that afternoon. Another church delivered a freshly-baked apple pie to my door the day after my first visit. After visits to other churches, I received a coupon to a local restaurant, ice-cream cone gift certificates, and even free Christian concert tickets. I felt like I was receiving bribes to come back. I never knew what I'd get from the next place!"

**How does your singles ministry personalize your outreach to newcomers?** Does your follow-up express interest in the visitor as a person with interests and needs, or is it an attempt to impress? You be the judge. Choose your methods thoughtfully, and be careful not to overdo!

tionally followed up on newcomers with a pastoral visit.

This information should affect your decision of who follows up your visitors. If you wish to involve the pastor or staff person who relates to your program, let him or her help train the follow-up team. But let the team itself be comprised of volunteers from your program who have the appropriate skills, rather than the clergy or staff.

### WHO SHOULD BE FOLLOWED-UP?

The newcomers who have most recently visited your singles program are the best prospects to reach. Their experience with your singles group is fresh, and your prompt card or phone call reaffirms their positive experiences. People who visited your singles ministry months ago and never returned should not be high priority to contact and should never receive repeated calls. First-time people vote with their feet. They will return to your program if they are interested. ◄

With practice and consistency, your follow-up can be useful. Keep it simple, keep it organized, and (along with everything else you do for single adults) maintain quality! And remember: if you don't have quality events, all the follow-up in the world won't bring attenders back. The best follow-up is always having the best possible "setup" for the event.

▶ See "Tools to Help You" (below) for a description of (Resources 19 and 20), two follow-up forms you may reproduce and use.

## TOOLS TO HELP YOU

Use the resources on the following pages to help you establish and maintain quality follow-up of newcomers to your single adults ministry events.

• **Resource 17, "Registration Sign-In Sheet"** *(Sample)* Duplicate and use this sheet to collect names and addresses of those who come to each singles ministry entry event.

• **Resource 18, "What to Say on the Phone"** *(Guidelines)* Use these guidelines to give you and your follow-up team ideas for making phone calls to newcomers.

• **Resource 19, " Follow-Up Record Sheet" and Resource 20, "Individual Follow-Up Report"** *(Samples)* These examples of forms can help you keep track of your newcomers and develop records of your follow-up contacts. (Give a copy of these resources to each person who is helping with follow-up.) Discuss these with your singles group and decide what works best for your situation.

# REGISTRATION SIGN-IN SHEET

Name of Event_____ Date_____

| NAME | ADDRESS/CITY/STATE/ZIP | PHONE | FIRST-TIMERS CHECK HERE |
|------|------------------------|-------|-------------------------|
|  |  |  |  |
|  |  |  |  |
|  |  |  |  |
|  |  |  |  |
|  |  |  |  |
|  |  |  |  |
|  |  |  |  |
|  |  |  |  |
|  |  |  |  |
|  |  |  |  |
|  |  |  |  |
|  |  |  |  |
|  |  |  |  |
|  |  |  |  |

# WHAT TO SAY ON THE PHONE

## GENERAL GUIDELINES

Are you calling someone who was a first-time visitor at one of your singles events? Decide the purposes of your call before you ever pick up the phone. Focus on these three simple messages:
- We're glad you came!
- Please join us again anytime!
- Can I answer any questions for you about our church or singles ministry?
  In most cases, your call should take no longer than two minutes.

### Example Follow-Up Call

"Hi! This is (*your name*) calling from the singles ministry at (*church's name*) Church. We wanted to thank you for attending our (*name of event*). Did you find it helpful or interesting?"

"We want you to know you're welcome at our single adult activities—or any church activities—anytime."

OPTIONAL: "One of our next events for singles will be our (*name of upcoming event*) on (*day or date*). It will be a good event, and we'd be glad to have you there."

"Are there any questions about our church or our singles program that I can answer for you?"

"Thanks again for coming!"

## "DON'TS" FOR MAKING FOLLOW-UP CALLS

- **DON'T** ask personal questions about divorce, ex-spouse, living location, or type of work the visitor does—and don't volunteer that information about yourself.

- **DON'T** insist on covering all the points suggested in the example above if the visitor seems impatient or in a hurry. Cheerfully convey the most important part of the message, "We're glad you came!" Then politely end the call.

- **DON'T** respond likewise if the person is rude or unfriendly. Keep a pleasant demeanor, no matter what.

## "DOS" FOR MAKING FOLLOW-UP CALLS

- **DO** pray for each visitor before calling, asking God to help you communicate clearly.

- **DO** be cheerful. A smile will be reflected in your voice.

# FOLLOW-UP RECORD SHEET

Event _____ Date of Event _____

**Our singles ministry's "follow-up" purpose is:** _____

_____

_____

_____

**Who will help do the follow-up?**

| Name | Phone | Name | Phone |
|------|-------|------|-------|
| 1. _____ | _____ | 5. _____ | _____ |
| 2. _____ | _____ | 6. _____ | _____ |
| 3. _____ | _____ | 7. _____ | _____ |
| 4. _____ | _____ | 8. _____ | _____ |

**To whom will the persons doing follow-up submit their follow-up reports?**

Name _____ Phone _____

**By what date should the contacts be completed?**_____

**What method(s) will be used?** (Check.) ❐ Mail ❐ Phone ❐ Home Visit

| Newcomer | Address | Phone | Contact Person |
|----------|---------|-------|----------------|
| 1. _____ | _____ _____ | _____ | _____ |
| 2. _____ | _____ _____ | _____ | _____ |
| 3. _____ | _____ _____ | _____ | _____ |
| 4. _____ | _____ _____ | _____ | _____ |
| 5. _____ | _____ _____ | _____ | _____ |

# INDIVIDUAL FOLLOW-UP REPORT

Visitor's Name _____ Phone _____

Address _____ ZIP _____

**Method of follow-up:**

❑ Postcard ❑ Note ❑ Letter ❑ Phone Call ❑ Answering Machine ❑ Home Visit

Date follow-up took place:_____

Brief Description: _____

_____

_____

_____

If contact was via phone or in person, was the response favorable? ❑ Yes ❑ No *(Briefly explain.)*

_____

_____

_____

Your name _____ Date _____

---

# INDIVIDUAL FOLLOW-UP REPORT

Visitor's Name _____ Phone _____

Address _____ ZIP _____

**Method of follow-up:**

❑ Postcard ❑ Note ❑ Letter ❑ Phone Call ❑ Answering Machine ❑ Home Visit

Date follow-up took place:_____

Brief Description: _____

_____

_____

_____

If contact was via phone or in person, was the response favorable? ❑ Yes ❑ No *(Briefly explain.)*

_____

_____

_____

Your name _____ Date _____

# Helping Single Adults Move toward Greater Commitment

REPRODUCIBLE RESOURCE AT THE END OF THIS CHAPTER

Part of your responsibility as a singles ministry leader is always to be in the process of building other leaders so that your single adult ministry leadership constantly replenishes itself. However, not all people who attend your events will become part of your program's leadership team. Many may not even be committed to coming on a regular basis. Some will come once or twice and never return.

Learning how to minister to singles includes understanding varying patterns of commitment levels and working within that framework. There is a dynamic component involved in working with single adult ministry, because a certain portion of your group's membership is always changing. Adult singles in today's society frequently undergo changes in relationships, jobs, geographical locations, finances, and even parenting styles. Flexibility is necessary to develop a singles program with a solid, consistent leadership core. At the same time, the program must offer enough elasticity for people to come and go without causing the loss of group identity or purpose.

The associate pastor of one large church emphatically stated that singles ministry was not possible in his congregation. "I spent three months enlisting a group of single adults to serve on a singles group task force and to commit to a two-year term. At the end of six months every one had either moved away, gotten involved in a serious relationship, married, or had schedule problems with their children that prevented them from serving anymore. I was back to ground zero! Why should I pour all my time into people who won't honor their terms of office?"

This minister was accustomed to working with the established committee structure of his congregation. Those committees required a several-year commitment and were usually filled with long-time church members. He did not understand the fluidity of a single adult facing life transitions from a divorce, the (sometimes) transient life-style of young adults, or the lack of time in a single parent's hectic schedule. He assumed that any unmarried person was automatically a good candidate for leadership in the church's new singles group. He had not learned how to discern which singles were ready for a leadership commitment and which were at earlier stages along the commitment journey.

There are two perspectives to understand when exploring the "journey of commitment" for single adults. The first is an overview of the general levels of commitment that usually occur among adults moving through your singles ministry. The second is a look at the underlying principles of why people make commitments to church involvement. By understanding these two areas, you can more comfortably work with the "inflow-outflow" nature of your singles group or programs and more effectively gear your singles ministry to help foster commitment.

## LEVELS OF COMMITMENT

Generally speaking, five basic categories of single adults exist as parts of your singles ministry. ◄

### 1. "Prospective attenders" category

This category includes all the single adults in your community and surrounding area. Entry level events are held especially for these people (see Chapter 4). This category is a large, significant group filled with many prospects—but sometimes singles ministries close themselves to these visitors by being self-focused rather than outwardly-focused. Unless points of entry into your singles ministry are intentionally aimed at this population, these people probably won't move into your singles group activities.

▶ Use Resource 21, "Commitment Levels," page 108, to help you evaluate the commitment level of your singles ministry attenders. It contains questions which can be used as discussion starters with your leadership team.

A biblical mandate encourages us to never lose sight of the prospects. Although Jesus constantly trained and nurtured His "leadership team" of disciples, He consistently reached out to those beyond His close circle. He held "entry events" like the large gathering at His Sermon on the Mount and the great predecessor to our church potluck dinners—His feeding of the five thousand with the loaves and fishes! (Matt. 14:13-21)

Besides the large events, Jesus also spent time explaining the purpose of His ministry and message to individuals and small groups of people. While He did spend time alone with His disciples for leadership development, He also created a steady diet of outreach opportunities for newcomers. In fact, the mandate of Christ's Great Commission (Matt. 28:18-20) is a statement about keeping ministry focused upon the "potentials" category.

### 2. "Perimeter people" category

"Perimeter people" are those who sporadically attend events and appear interested in singles activities but don't seem particularly committed to the program.

For a variety of reasons, a certain number of individuals will always remain perimeter people. For example, some may be members of another church that does not have a singles group—and while they enjoy attending yours upon occasion, they remain committed to their home congregation. Others may have schedule conflicts, be struggling with faith issues, or have a current romantic relationship with someone outside the church. Still others may find that your singles activities only periodically address their needs or interests.

Unfortunately, many singles ministries spend significant time and energy pursuing long-term perimeter people with repeated follow-up. They often hope that "if we keep after them, they'll come around!" But this results in either a singles group full of individuals who feel pushed and prodded into coming or a frustrated, discouraged follow-up team. Neither situation is healthy!

Realize that perimeter people exist in every singles ministry. Honor them, remembering that some may move from this category into one of more steady attendance and even leadership.

### 3. "Regular attenders" category

These people appear at most or all events. They see benefit in the singles activities and perhaps even gain significantly from them in the areas of healing and personal or spiritual growth. Regular attenders identify themselves as belonging to the singles ministry, but usually see themselves only as participants and receivers. They sometimes volunteer to help, but only on an event-to-event basis.

Regular attenders may arrive early and will usually help set up chairs or lay out refreshments if asked to lend a hand. But they usually refuse to serve on a regular committee, commit ahead of time to help plan events, or be part of anything with a long-term clause attached.

Many single adults who attend your programs will be comfortable when they reach this point. You will learn to discern

---

## Following-Up Perimeter People

**Is any follow-up appropriate for perimeter people?** Yes, when they are first- or second-time visitors. After that, the best follow-up will occur at your events—by offering quality activities filled with friendliness.

**Don't ignore the perimeter people** because you'll want to be ready when some indicate interest in becoming more involved.

who in this category have probably reached their full involvement potential and who are moving toward the next levels of commitment.

### 4. "Willing volunteers" category

These people may be relatively new to the program, or they may have been around for some time. They will volunteer ahead of time (or agree when invited) to bring cookies, be greeters, make posters, or complete other assigned tasks.

Willing volunteers are task-oriented and enjoy "episodic volunteer" opportunities (a short-term commitment with a specific beginning and end to the task). They usually want clear directions. Willing volunteers may sometimes assist leaders, but are often reluctant to assume a full leadership responsibility. Persons in this category fit perfectly in involvements like going on short-term mission projects, serving as small group leaders for a six- or eight-week divorce recovery workshop, or making follow-up phone calls after a specific event.

Willing volunteers are usually "testing the waters" in regard to their increasing involvement in your singles ministry. Some will move to the leadership team level after one or two volunteer experiences. Others will take longer to decide whether or not to make a greater commitment.

Some in the "willing volunteer" category perceive themselves as more committed than they really are. No matter what enthusiasm level a single adult expresses in moving through the five described categories, everyone should complete at least one assignment in this category before moving onto the leadership team. Short-term commitments are a good way for persons to discover whether they really want a longer-term responsibility in your program or are capable of sustaining one. Jesus stressed this principle in the parable of the talents—the person who proved himself faithful with a few things was put in charge of many things (Matt. 25:21).

Willing volunteers especially need to receive personal thanks and public appreciation for their work. Their enthusiasm will wane if their contributions go unnoticed or increase if they feel their contribution has been recognized.

### 5. "Leadership team" category

These individuals form the committed center of your singles ministry. They have a vested interest in the development of the singles program. They have a high level of dedication as volunteers and are usually the decision-makers and the trendsetters for the rest of the ministry. A few of the leadership team individuals will be visionaries. All should be willing to take responsibility and authority.

Of all the five categories, the leadership team people must be able to look outward to the edges of your singles ministry and make sure regular entry points are offered for the perimeter people.

One unique characteristic of developing a leadership team is that because of the changeability in the lives of single adults, the leadership team makeup may also reflect frequent change. No matter how committed, a leadership team member sometimes faces a personal transition (such as marriage, job transfer, or child custody) which forces him or her to reduce or discontinue leadership involvement. Because of this, it is essential to keep track of those who are moving through the categories toward the leadership team level and continually add new team members to keep the leadership strong.

### PRINCIPLES THAT MOVE PEOPLE TOWARD GREATER COMMITMENT

What draws people into greater commitment to the church and to your singles ministry? Their personal perceptions about your ministry and the characteristics of that ministry facilitate increased involvement.

### Single adults' personal perceptions

Three vital perceptions about your ministry motivate people to get more involved. The first two are identified by George Barna.[1]

*1. The ministry is high quality.* People become committed to their church programs because *they have found what they believe is a "high quality" ministry,* executed with a spirit of excellence.

*2. The ministry meets felt needs.* People become committed to their church programs because *the church or ministry uses a "felt-needs" approach.* They are convinced their church or ministry addresses the most relevant issues in their lives. Their enthusiasm about the quality of their church's ministry, coupled with the dramatic impact of the ministry upon their personal lives, motivates people to commit deeply to the vision of leadership and to extend the mission of the church to others.

---

*Is the felt-needs approach viable for the Church? According to George Barna, some ministry leaders fear that if the church pays too much attention to what people feel they need, proclaiming the Gospel will be compromised. Yet healthy, growing ministries across the country have disproved this thesis. People are seeking significant solutions to their deepest struggles. A needs-based, Christ-centered outreach helps apply the truth of Scripture to people's lives in a targeted way. This encourages spiritual growth and ensures effective ministry.[2]*

---

*3. The ministry offers help, home, and hope.* Kennon Callahan, Eugene Brice, and other church growth experts have pointed out a third set of factors that contribute to the commitment level of church attenders. Basically, people look for three things from their church:

*Help*—compassion from God and other Christians.

*Home*—the sense of community, relationships, a feeling of being where we belong in God's family.

*Hope*—the conviction that the church is guiding us and reaching God's full potential for our lives.

Church ministries that provide opportunities for attenders to experience these three aspects fan the flames of commitment.

In summary, single adults are motivated along the journey of their commitment at the same rate at which they develop the following convictions about the ministry in which they are involved:

• The belief that their singles ministry

---

## Help, Home, Hope

*What do "help," "home," and "hope" look like in a singles ministry?* Here are some examples:

**HELP**—support groups (grief, single parents, divorce, addictions, and other life issues); singles service teams; short-term mission trips; food pantry for singles in crisis; educational classes on relevant or self-help topics.

**HOME**—fellowship events such as potluck dinners or parties on holidays; social and recreational activities; small group experiences; corporate worship opportunities; singles ministry retreats or conferences.

**HOPE**—Sunday classes; Bible study small groups; positive "image" projected by the singles ministry; worship opportunities; healing ministries of divorce or grief recovery.

is a "high quality" organization.

• The belief that their singles ministry helps provide answers to their own deeply-felt questions and solutions to their life issues.

• The belief that involvement in their singles ministry can help them experience help, home, and hope.

**Characteristics of your singles ministry**

In addition to key personal perceptions, certain characteristics of your ministry can also move people toward greater commitment.

Some people will always be perimeter people. Others will stay "regular attenders." Don't exhaust yourself or your follow-up team by trying to coax these people. Remember: *It's easier to restrain a fanatic than to raise a corpse.* Invest your time and energy in cultivating people who are excited about your singles ministry rather than in trying to revive those who aren't!

Look for the people who show signs of wanting to become more involved. You will find them in the "regular attenders" and "willing volunteers" categories. Potential "leadership team" people will emerge if your singles program is one in which they can easily become more involved.

The following singles ministry characteristics may help people in your group move toward greater commitment levels.

*1. The current volunteer leaders of your program should be friendly, clearly identified, and accessible to the people at your events.* This lets those who are interested in your work know who to talk to about the group's vision and what being part of the leadership team is like. Letting people know who is responsible gives potential leaders role models to observe. Encourage leaders not only to visit with the people they know, but to circulate. This will enhance their accessibility to newcomers and help them get acquainted with more people.

At a large church in Indianapolis, Indiana, attenders of singles events have a choice of three colors when it comes to name tags. Wearing one color represents "first-time visitor." Another color is for those who consider themselves "regular attenders." Those on the singles ministry leadership teams wear the third color. This method helps everyone identify who the "resource people" are. This also alerts everyone to the presence of first-timers who might need help finding a room or getting answers to their questions.

NOTE: The current leaders should always act as the "eyes and ears" of your singles ministry, finding out who is interested and ready to move toward greater involvement. They should invite others to help whenever possible. (For example, "early birds" to an event may secretly want something to do, but they are afraid to volunteer. Leaders should be alert to this and offer them a job.)

*2. Your program should provide clear, easy paths to becoming more committed within the singles program.* To prevent the complaint, "I'd like to become more involved, but I don't know where to start!" successful singles ministries give participants clear information about existing volunteer opportunities and contact people.

Listing committees and their responsibilities in your newsletters or flyers, for example, gives people a better idea of how their talents might fit into the program picture. Then when you invite someone to become more involved in a specific area, that person already has some understanding of how the suggested responsibility fits into the overall program. Also, it gives everyone with specific talents (whether personally contacted or not) a chance to examine the possibilities of volunteering for a specific work area.

Make sure you clearly explain what skills or expertise you need for various volunteer opportunities. Clearly written job descriptions for each leadership position are invaluable.

**3. Your singles ministry should have classes, groups, committees, or other specialized events that are continually being created or starting anew.** A frustrating part of being new to a group is trying to break into the "closed" fellowship of an already-established company of people. Nothing stifles the wish to get involved more than feeling "shut out." People are more likely to feel ownership and commitment when they have a chance to get in on the ground floor of a new group, event, or class.

Your ministry needs to be aware of how quickly groups become "closed." To offset this, you must have new activities beginning on a continual, regular basis. Do not fall into the trap of thinking fellowship groups which have been in existence for even a few months are adequate "open doors" for newcomers. Groups "close" in just a few meetings—sometimes by the second time they meet. Remember and practice the principle of good entry events as explained in Chapter 4.

**4. Your program should encourage people to move toward small group settings.** Church growth consultant Lyle Schaller says that if a newcomer to a church makes even a handful of friends in the congregation, he or she will never leave that church.

If you believe this can apply to singles ministries, you will prioritize creating small group opportunities where individuals can build community, establish friendships, and grow spiritually as well as emotionally. A positive small-group experience cements the commitment of its members to the overall program and equips them to enthusiastically invite friends to attend the program.

"Small-group opportunity" does not always mean a Bible study. Small group settings also include volleyball or softball teams, "interest" groups (gatherings of like-minded singles who enjoy games, travel, reading, sports, cultural events, eating out, special hobbies, or other interests), "growth groups" to discuss life issues, and book study/discussion groups. Be creative!

A small group is a group that's small enough for everyone to get to know one another. Whether with only a few, or as many as twenty, an effective small group of people form community, support, and friendships.

**5. Try to be sure all discussion group materials used in your programs are high quality and relevant to the lives of the participants.** Nothing builds more interest and commitment to your program than when participants encounter relevant information presented in a life-changing way. Lackluster study materials leave people uncertain about whether or not your ministry is worthwhile and will ultimately convince them that it isn't.

*What characterizes good study material?*

• *It's theologically sound.* (Ask your pastor to evaluate the material if you're uncertain).

• *It's practical and relevant for daily life.*

---

## Scheduling New Entry Points

**How often should you schedule new entry points?** Only you and your leadership team can assess what is appropriate for your church, your community, and the overall context of your singles ministry. Whether it's twice a month or once a quarter, don't schedule more entry events than you can create with quality and a spirit of excellence. A poorly-executed entry event is worse than none at all.

• *It's interesting to those in your singles program.*

• *It's peppered with questions for group discussion.* (Or it's designed so the leader can easily create discussion questions).

• *It's easy for the leader to prepare to lead.*

---

**Broaden your choice of resources. You don't always have to use lessons specifically written for single adults. Materials dealing with general "adult life" issues can be very useful and appealing.**

---

How should you find study material?

• *Check the bibliography in this book.*

• *Ask your pastor to recommend some material.*

• *Ask the singles ministry participants for suggestions.*

• *Peruse possibilities at Christian and general bookstores, as well as the local library.*

• *Ask leaders of other singles ministries what their participants liked.*

• *Check the listing of resources in the* National Single Adult Ministries Resource Directory *produced by Singles Ministry Resources* (available by calling 1-800-487-4-SAM [USA]).

**6. The group leaders or teachers in your classes and small groups must be well-prepared.** Your volunteer leaders do not have to be professional speakers or teachers, but they do need to be equipped for their job. Offer them training—whether by your pastor, by an effective leader in your congregation, or by group study of leadership and discussion group leader skills.

A group leader must understand small group dynamics. Emphasize to these leaders that nothing destroys a group faster than a poorly-prepared leader or a leader who tries to "wing it." The privilege of leadership includes the responsibility to prepare.

At the outset, establish the length of the "term of obligation" for each leader by setting beginning and ending dates. This prevents "burnout" of a teacher who feels forced into teaching longer than desired—and gives your group a chance to replace an ineffective teacher.

Be patient with volunteer leaders and teachers. They need time and practice to hone their skills. For books to help them improve their understanding of small groups and classes, see the bibliography in this book.

**7. Your ministry should occasionally offer retreats, conferences, or training events for your singles to attend together.** Positive group experiences such as these can build deep commitment. They usually "bond" those who have attended and create among them a shared vision for your program.

Many denominations have regional or national single adult conferences or training events (or singles events for personal enrichment) at least once a year. A number of interdenominational events are also held annually across the country to give leaders a chance for more training. Your singles ministry might also create its own weekend "retreat" for leadership building or creating community.

**8. Your ministry should routinely help participants find ways to use their talents and skills in the ministry.** Helping people "find their places" to volunteer in your singles ministry is essential to greater involvement and commitment.

The next chapter of this book (Chapter 8) contains suggestions on how to help build and equip volunteer involvement. Read on for ideas, worksheets, interview forms, and other crucial information on how to create a pattern of healthy volunteerism.

## HANG ON TO YOUR FOCUS

Above everything else, remember your singles program is not for everyone. Not everyone will find personal needs met in your singles ministry, nor will everyone think you have the greatest singles ministry in town. If you are doing your job right, your singles program will offer meaning and purpose for the single adults you have targeted. And those singles will spread the word about all the good things that are happening. Be content with doing your program well, and don't compare your ministry with others.

## TOOLS TO HELP YOU

**Resource 21, "Commitment Levels"** *(Discussion Sheet)* is designed to help you evaluate the composition of your singles ministry attendance. Use it as a discussion starter with your planning group or leadership team.

# COMMITMENT LEVELS

Discuss the five levels-of-commitment categories in the chart below, informally estimating what percentage of your singles ministry is comprised of each category. Then discuss the questions that follow.

## FIVE LEVELS OF COMMITMENT

| | |
|---|---|
| **PROSPECTIVE ATTENDERS** _____Percent | All single adults in your church, neighborhood, city, and area. |
| **PERIMETER PEOPLE** _____Percent | Singles who attend sporadically and seem interested but do not see themselves as committed or obligated to the group. |
| **REGULAR ATTENDERS** _____Percent | Singles who attend regularly, view themselves as participants or receivers, and may help on an event-to-event basis. |
| **WILLING VOLUNTEERS** _____Percent | Singles who agree to short-term volunteer responsibilities and may serve on committees but do not want full leadership responsibilities. |
| **LEADERSHIP TEAM** _____Percent | Singles who form the committed "center" of the singles ministry; dedicated; willing to make decisions, accept responsibility and authority, and share the vision. |

## DISCUSSION QUESTIONS

**1. Are we satisfied with the distribution of categories in our singles ministry? Why or why not?**

*(continued)*

**2. How would we (realistically) like the distribution to look one, two, and five years from now?**

• One year from now?

• Two years from now?

• Five years from now?

**3. How can we help people move further along their "journey of commitment"?**

**4. What have we learned through our discussion of this chart?**

**5. What is our practical "game plan" derived from this discussion?**

# Building and Enabling Volunteer Involvement

REPRODUCIBLE RESOURCES AT THE END OF THIS CHAPTER

The last chapter described the "journey of commitment" single adults in your singles ministry events will travel. As mentioned, adult singles tend to move toward increasing involvement if:

- They believe that their singles ministry is "high quality."
- They believe the singles ministry provides answers and solutions to their own life questions and issues.
- They believe that involvement in the singles ministry can help them find opportunities to experience *help* (healing, learning, and personal growth), *home* (fellowship, responsibility, significance, affirmation, community), and *hope* (spiritual development and maturity).

The greater the extent to which your single adults encounter these factors, the more positive they will become about volunteer involvement. This chapter will help you learn how to be a "relational leader" who is intentional in the recruitment and enablement of volunteers. Helping volunteers find significance, purpose, and satisfaction builds their commitment to the ministry. This is essential to your effectiveness as a leader. If you learn the "art" of recruiting and enabling an effective volunteer corps, your singles ministry will be healthy and growing.

At this point, it is important to note that "ministry success" does not necessarily mean numerical growth. It means growth of your volunteers in personal, relational, and spiritual maturity. If you build and nurture your volunteer leadership, the result will be a proliferation of volunteers who feel significantly engaged in ministry and are learning how to develop healthy relationships with others and with God.

The volunteer leaders in your singles ministry should be people who, through personal and spiritual growth, model for others the example of a godly and moral life-style. The most effective volunteers will be those who have learned to honor God's call to "walk worthy" of the privilege of servant leadership.

## RECRUITING "INTENTIONALLY"

**Why not recruit just anyone for leadership roles?**

Intentional volunteer recruitment and enablement in your singles ministry is founded upon the following biblical mandates.

---

*"We have different gifts, according to the grace given us. If a man's gift is prophesying, let him use it in proportion to his faith. If it is serving, let him serve; if it is teaching, let him teach; if it is encouraging, let him encourage; if it is contributing to the needs of others, let him give generously; if it is leadership, let him govern diligently; if it is showing mercy, let him do it cheerfully."*
—ROMANS 12:6-8

---

## Every Volunteer is a Partner in Leadership

Every volunteer in your singles ministry, no matter what size the task, is part of your program's leadership. Everyone who contributes time and energy to the creation of an event or activity for your singles group is a valuable partner in the ministry leadership.

This chapter refers to all those who help in the ministry leadership as "volunteers," recognizing that some will undertake small, specific tasks and others will assume planning, organizing, and supervising greater responsibilities. It is designed to help you learn how to enlist and prepare all types of volunteers—whether for a one-time task or for a comprehensive leadership position.

> *"Each one should use whatever gift he has received to serve others, faithfully administering God's grace in its various forms."* —I PETER 4:10

Apply these scriptural guidelines when filling volunteer openings. Rather than just finding "warm bodies" to fill a niche—and thinking the ministry will fall apart or fail if you don't—make your singles ministry a place where people are helped to use and develop their special gifts or talents. The ministry becomes unique and effective when it's based on the gifts of people involved rather than on another church's program model that may call for gifts your people don't have.

**What are the benefits of intentional recruitment?**

One way you benefit by recruiting a broad base of volunteers is that *it helps your single adults become personally involved in what is happening.* Programs feel like a "spectator sport" for those who never do more than simply attend the events. And those attenders will remain spectators unless they are invited to move toward increased involvement.

By directly involving a person in your ministry, you succeed in a second facet of recruiting volunteers: *spreading ownership, authority, and a sense of purpose.* The ministry will not become vital and life-giving to the participants unless the program decisions and ministry belong to them. As long as it is your program, your ideas, and you doing all the work, the ministry will extend only as far as your own energy can reach. Ideally, you should instead assume the role of resource person, visionary, teacher, coach, and trainer of others to share with you in the ministry joys and labor.

A third benefit to be gained by intentionally recruiting volunteers is that *it helps people grow personally.* You will find it almost miraculous to see individuals, when invited to assume leadership responsibilities, be transformed in their confidence, self-worth, and faith. If one of your ministry goals is to help people grow personally and spiritually, the most effective way to achieve this is by recruiting them as volunteers.

**Why do some leaders fail to recruit help?**

If your singles group seems to have a shortage of volunteers, it may be that you have not used informed, focused, inten-

---

## Characteristics of Growing Churches

The Barna Research Group studied a large group of growing churches across the country. The goal was to identify characteristics those churches shared in common that set them apart from plateaued or declining congregations.

"One of the actions that most clearly separated growing churches from stagnant churches was the willingness of the growing bodies to accept people for who they were. Rather than take persons who volunteered their services and plug them into the most gaping hole that exists at the moment, user-friendly churches first helped people determine what God had called them to do. They believed that each person had an area of giftedness, and they strove to use that person's talents and skills in those areas. . . . By employing volunteers in the areas in which they are gifted, the probability of burnout, disenchantment with the church, disappointment with either the role they are asked to play or with the outcome of their own performance, is minimized. What tended to happen was that those involved in the ministry in areas of their own giftedness actually enjoyed what they did and gained a sense of fulfillment from their involvement." —George Barna[1]

▶ For positive and effective ways to approach potential volunteers, see pages 116 and 117. These points are also summarized on Resource 22, "Volunteer Interest Interview," page 122.

tional energy to recruit individuals whose skills match the ministry needs. There are some basic reasons why many ministry leaders consciously or unconsciously avoid an ongoing procedure of intentionally recruiting volunteers.

*1. Lone Ranger complex.* Many leaders fail to recruit because they think it's easier to do it themselves than to get someone to help. Harried ministry leaders with long "to do" lists often decide it is more timesaving to go ahead and make fifteen phone calls, for example, than to recruit a caller, explain the purpose of the calls, and together plan an appropriate message and over-the-phone approach. An additional challenge is getting the list of names and phone numbers to the volunteer caller.

If you are a church staff member or lay leader, you may routinely feel pushed into becoming this type of "manager" of details, rather than being an enabling leader. With too much work to do, you may find yourself frantically trying to accomplish as much as possible by the most energy-saving route. Time for training volunteers does not always fit into your managerial-style schedule.

*2. Fear of rejection.* Many leaders also avoid recruiting volunteers because they are *afraid of rejection*. No one likes to be told *no*, but part of finding the right person for the job includes receiving negative as well as affirmative responses. Sometimes recruiters virtually ensure receiving a no response from those they contact simply by the way that they ask.◀

*3. Fear of losing control.* Like it or not, the biggest reason many leaders find it hard to recruit and organize volunteers is that *it involves giving away ownership, authority, and responsibility.*

Delegating is difficult because it defies the natural bent of human nature. Inside all of us who are in leadership is a fear of forfeiting control! We want it our way. We're afraid of failure. If we are responsible for the program, we want to make sure it's done "right." We may even believe that no one can do it as well as we can.

This is a common cause of leadership burnout—leaders refusing to give away the ownership and responsibility of programs become overloaded. Does this describe you at times? Rather than empower others to share leadership, do you end up hanging onto the control and authority until you nearly lose heart and energy for any ministry at all?

In today's church, unfortunately, many ministries are "managed by managers" rather than led by leaders. To see spiritual growth and development, do not manage the singles ministry by hierarchy! Instead, develop a *relational leadership style* that defines your role as coach, "gift-finder," enabler, trainer, and supporter.

## BEING A RELATIONAL LEADER

**What is your role as a relational leader?**

Your role in the relational leadership style of ministry should ideally be defined by these responsibilities:

---

### Hierarchical vs. Relational Leadership[2]

**What are some differences between hierarchical managerial and relational leadership?**

| Hierarchical | Relational |
|---|---|
| Power divided | Power created |
| Power allocated | Power unlimited |
| Division of "turfs" | Building a team |
| Ownership by the few | Ownership by the many |
| Creativity stifled | Creativity encouraged |
| Planning done by one | Planning done by a team |

**1. Dream and share vision with the people in the program.** Too often, the vision for the ministry gets buried under the urgent, day-to-day tasks, and little time is spent developing and instilling the dream in others. Talk with the volunteers and participants of your singles program to hear their ideas and establish the direction of the ministry. Keeping the "big picture" in mind is the cornerstone of every successful singles program. ▶

To share the vision, you might schedule a periodic weekend or half-day retreat with volunteer teams from your singles ministry, providing relaxed time to think and dream together. Camaraderie will develop between all of you, which increases the sense of teamwork and ownership. For example, a good time to do a retreat is when there is a turnover in the membership of your dream team or leadership team. Some singles ministries hold a retreat every six months to refresh and renew their sense of mission.

If a getaway retreat is impossible, meet with volunteers individually (or in small groups) for coffee. This is an excellent setting for sharing vision, building dreams, and fostering relationships.

**2. Assume the role of "gift finder" rather than manager.** A "gift finder" is a leader who helps others discover their gifts and find ways to use them. A floundering ministry is often filled with individuals who don't know what their gifts are and don't have anyone helping them identify and employ their talents.

One singles ministry worker carries a small notebook and pen to every singles event. She observes and interacts with the participants, jotting down the names of those she sees as potential volunteers and the gifts she believes they might have. Later, she contacts each with an invitation to become involved in the capacities she thinks might appeal to them. Together, she and the volunteers clarify where their interests lie and what equipping or training might help each feel worthwhile, important, and competent in the volunteer responsibility. She is a good example of how a singles ministry leader can encourage increased involvement.

**3. Be accessible to the people in the singles ministry.** Being accessible is another key characteristic for the relational singles leader. This does not imply you must receive phone calls from participants any time of the day or night. Boundaries are necessary! But people must know when and where you are normally available for their visits, phone calls, and questions—and volunteers must feel confident that you will return their calls. Nothing kills enthusiasm more quickly than a leader who is chronically unpredictable, unavailable, and unreliable for support and information.

**4. Give responsibility, ownership, and authority to others.** When a singles group lacks volunteers, the leader usually has a stranglehold on all the power and authority. Ask yourself: *Am I primarily committed to getting people to do what I want them to do—or am I committed to accomplishing our vision as a team?*

A laywoman began a singles support group which met monthly in the church fellowship hall. Each month, she arrived early to make coffee, lay out special cookies she had baked, decorate the registration area, and place centerpieces on each table.

She occasionally convinced a friend or two to come early to help her set up. But after two years, she had become completely frustrated with the group of about thirty people. *After all,* she reasoned, *it isn't fair that I must always decorate and provide special refreshments. No one ever seems to care much about taking their turns at these jobs.*

She was surprised (and dismayed) when anonymous evaluation forms completed by the group revealed that no one cared if they had special cookies or if the

◀ Refer to the bibliography, page 190, for other excellent resources that can help you become a more effective leader.

registration area was decorated. They were primarily interested in the fellowship, study, and discussion. The "extras" she had provided (with increasing resentment) were incidentals to everyone else, and no one cared if those aspects were discontinued.

This is a prime example of a leader who is committed to his or her own agenda and tries to get others to help with it, rather than giving the responsibility of the event to others (who might not share the same perceptions of what makes a successful event). Releasing a death grip on total authority and responsibility is sometimes the hardest but most important task of a relational leader.

**5. *Be a decision-supporter and a "back slapper."*** Verbally appreciating people is crucial in nurturing volunteers. If you give authority and decision-making freedom to volunteers, support them, guide them in their decisions and plans, and encourage their sense of accomplishment by affirming a job well done.

### What's the best way to ask people to volunteer?

The key to establishing a successful and consistent flow of volunteers in your singles program is carefully planning how you will recruit and prepare your volunteers. ◄

The most common way for church ministries to recruit volunteers is to pass around a sheet and have someone announce, "We need some volunteers, so please sign up!" Another traditional method is to put a few sentences in the church bulletin or newsletter, asking for volunteers. Even though these seem like acceptable ways to recruit, they are actually some of the least effective ways to find volunteers.

Why? When a blanket invitation is given for anyone to step forward, people immediately assume the job is not particularly important. *After all,* they reason, *anyone can do it.* Who wants to volunteer for a task that anyone can do or that no one else *wants* to do? Another drawback to blanket invitations is that the same people volunteer repeatedly. The sense of ownership becomes very strong among the same few people.

***The crucial factor is to represent each responsibility in your singles program as being vitally important and to carefully recruit the person you will invite to fulfill each task.*** People rise to the occasion when asked to assume a job they believe is significant. Consider a person's gifts and talents, and approach him or her accordingly.

Some singles ministries have job descriptions, and volunteers are asked to fill out a simple interest interview form. ◄

Some ministries routinely offer personality inventory or spiritual gift tests to help people understand which volunteer tasks they might enjoy. (See list of resources on page 117.)

If new people understand that your group is serious about volunteers, their attitudes will be different. They will expect an invitation to assume responsibility. It may take time to revamp your group's (and your own) approach to and mind-set about volunteerism, but it is worth the work.

### What do you say to potential volunteers?

Do you ever avoid inviting people to volunteer because you aren't sure what to say and how to say it?

Offering an invitation is not difficult, but it does call for some thought and the personal belief that what you're asking the volunteer to do is a worthwhile task. Keep the following guidelines in mind as you approach volunteers with possible tasks they might do.

***1. Never apologize for inviting a volunteer to help.*** Don't say, "I know you are probably too busy to help us, but I'd like to ask anyway—." By apologizing, you

► See Resource 22, "Volunteer Interest Interview," page 122. This useful tool can help clarify the interest and skill areas of those who wish to volunteer.

► Resource 23, "Volunteer Recruitment Worksheet," page 124, will help you plan and prepare for recruiting volunteers.

communicate that the volunteer surely has something more important to do or that what you're asking is not worthwhile. Make your invitation to volunteer positive, simple, and straightforward. ▶

*2. Communicate that the task is worthwhile.* Don't downplay the responsibility of the task you are inviting the volunteer to do. People want to feel their involvement is important and needed.

*3. Represent the parameters of the task realistically and fairly.*

Three things a volunteer usually wants to know:

• *Will this job be meaningful?* Will I feel a sense of significance?

• *Will I have authority and structure?* What is the chain of command? Will I have the freedom to get things done?

• *What about training?* How will I effectively learn what I've been asked to do?

*4. Remember that each contact with a prospective volunteer is a ministry opportunity in itself.*

A church staff worker in charge of a large program hated phoning to recruit volunteers. She complained that it took too long to get through each call.

"Sometimes they say yes or no right away, and sometimes not until the end of the phone call," she said. "But even when they say no, they want me to listen to some long story about their work, their children, their finances, or something that seems irrelevant to what I'm asking. I wish I knew how to find out right off if a person is going to say yes. Then I could get off the phone and onto the next call."

This worker demonstrated the "managerial" style of doing church work. Predictably, her volunteer pool dwindled because those who worked with her felt unappreciated, unimportant, and uncared for. Her unwillingness to extend a compassionate ear and kind attitude gave her programs a negative image. The effectiveness of her work did not take an upward swing until she began to see the value of interacting and building relationships with the volunteers as a crucial part of ministry. She began to change from being primarily "task-oriented" to becoming more "relationship-oriented."

Always remember the importance of caring for the individuals you invite to volunteer, whether they say yes or no. God's love is extended through your willingness to listen, to support, and to understand those with whom you minister. Your willingness to form a relation-

◀ For a handy overview of "What to Say to a Prospective Volunteer," refer to page 188 in the Appendix.

---

## Possible Tests to Use with Volunteer Leaders

The personality inventory test found in the book, *Please Understand Me: Character and Temperament Types,* by David W. Keirsey, Marilyn Bates, Stephen E. Montgomery (ed.). Del Mar, CA: Prometheus Nemesis Book Co., 1978.

Resources for helping your leaders discover their spiritual gifts:

• *Giving the Body a Lift by Using Your Spiritual Gift,* by Randy Petersen and Don Cousins. (Elgin, IL: David C. Cook Ministry Resources, 1993).

• *Discovering Your Spiritual Gifts in Small Groups,* by Paul Ford. (Pasadena, CA: Fuller Evangelistic Association, 1991).

• *Spiritual Gifts Implementation,* by Bob and Janet Logan. (Pasadena, CA: Fuller Evangelistic Association, 1989).

• *Networking Serving Seminar: Equipping Those Who Are Seeking to Serve,* by Bruce Bugbee. Pasadena, CA: Fuller Evangelistic Association, 1989.

For more information on the spiritual gifts tests, contact the Charles Fuller Institute of Evangelism and Church Growth in Pasadena, California at 800-235-2222 or 818-449-0425.

ship with volunteers and to appreciate their work and family situations will strengthen and empower them for service—and help them to feel cared for as persons.

### GETTING VOLUNTEERS OFF TO A GOOD START

You can help volunteers get off to a good start by giving them the proper "setup" and proper "follow-through." A written job description helps in both areas. ◄

► See Resource 24, "Volunteer Ministry Position Description," page 125.

**Setup**

These ingredients assist proper volunteer setup:

*1. Help the volunteer understand the overall purpose of the ministry and where he or she fits in.* Some volunteers may be fairly new to your singles ministry. Help them see the "big picture" and the part they will play in it. Remind them that, as a volunteer, they are part of the leadership of your program. Every volunteer job, no matter the degree or responsibility, helps provide leadership and direction for your overall singles ministry.

*2. Explain the organizational struc-ture of the church and give information about how to work within it.* Many volunteers become frustrated because they don't know how to go through the "red tape" to accomplish their tasks. Answer questions like these:

• *Where can I find the chairs for the meeting?*

• *How do I turn on the air conditioner?*

• *What are the church bulletin or newsletter deadlines for publicity and to whom do I submit announcements?*

Carefully consider the particular task you have asked the volunteer to do, and make sure you answer the types of questions which will probably arise as that person carries out the task. These details can be included on the "Volunteer Ministry Description" form for easy reference.

*3. Let each volunteer know what is expected.* If your singles ministry does not use a ministry description form, encourage each volunteer to write down his or her own outline of responsibility after you have discussed the job. Make a copy for the singles ministry files. Refer to it when helping any substitute under-

---

## Recruiting Phrases—Winners and Losers

When recruiting volunteers, use phrases that will emphasize the fact that the task at hand is worthwhile and important.

| DO SAY | DON'T SAY |
|---|---|
| These simple, clear phrases do belong in what you say to a volunteer: | These phrases do not belong in your invitation to a potential volunteer. |
| • "We are looking for someone with real gifts in this area for this responsibility." | • "I know you're busy, but—" |
| • "Do you have interests in this area?" | • "Would you mind doing a little thing for our program?" |
| • "How can we help you contribute some of your talents to the singles ministry programs?" | • "We're desperate for new people to help us. We really need you to say yes." |
| • "Would you like to—?" (instead of, "Could you—?" or "Would you be willing to—?") | • "Could you at all possibly do this?" |
| • "I've noticed you seem to be gifted in this area—" | • "We can't find anybody else to do it—" |

---

stand his or her responsibilities when taking over for the regular volunteer. It also helps you describe the job when you must recruit a new volunteer.

**4. Let your volunteers know what they can expect from you.** Many leaders fail at this point. Volunteers are often bewildered about their extent of authority and what role their leader/director (you) will play. You help volunteers tremendously by stating, simply and plainly, what they can expect from you.

• *At what times will you be available for them to call you?*

• *Will you provide special training? When?*

• *Do you plan to take care of any details of the project yourself?*

• *Will you meet with them regularly to plan, pray, or assist them?*

• *Will you be present at the activity for which they are volunteering to help?*

Sometimes *leaders* are the reason that volunteers do poorly at their tasks—leaders define what they expect of the volunteers, but do not communicate what the volunteers can expect of them.

### Follow-through

These are specific tenets of proper follow-through on your part as the leader which will help volunteers succeed:

**1. Do for the volunteers what you said you would do.** If you promised to supply paper cups and napkins, be certain you carry through! If you've said you would call, be sure you make that call. You cannot expect your volunteers to be any more reliable than you are.

**2. Compliment your volunteers.** The greatest encouragement is to be affirmed for a "labor of love." Give this affirmation to all who share their time and energy. Never hesitate to reward volunteers—by public recognition and by personal words of appreciation.

**3. Be available to encourage and assist them with problem solving.** Nothing discourages a volunteer more than to feel that those on the staff or program leadership are not supportive. The leader's job includes providing encouragement and offering problem-solving support. Do not abandon a volunteer or expect that person to know everything about how to accomplish a task without support or training. Follow up the volunteers regularly once they begin, and let them know you stand with them.

**4. Invest time and energy in your volunteers.** You can do this in many ways—regular meetings, phone calls, a note or postcard, or a casual conversation in the parking lot. *If you skip this step, your volunteers will "burn out" and move out of your singles ministry at an alarming rate!*

Never lose sight of this foundational truth: *programs exist for the people—not the reverse!* When you try desperately to find a handful of volunteers just for the sake of keeping a specific program alive, you have tried to make the cart pull the horse. Care about persons as individuals and see the programs as existing solely for the purpose of building and developing their lives through significant volunteer involvement.

## DISCERNING WHEN VOLUNTEERS HAVE SUCCEEDED

Do you ever confuse *work styles* with *volunteer effectiveness*? It's easy for leaders to do. If a volunteer doesn't accomplish the task in a particular style (usually *your* preferred work style!), you may tend to think the volunteer is not doing the job correctly.

However, most tasks can be accomplished in many ways. As a good leader, you should define the boundaries of a task. Then give permission, power, and support to the volunteer to figure out the best way to accomplish the responsibility.

These following guidelines can help you objectively assess the productivity of a volunteer, task force, or committee:

*1. Is the work done in harmony with the overall mission or purpose statement of the singles ministry?*

*2. Is the work done on time?*

*3. Is the work done in such a way that it enhances the whole project or program, rather than interferes with other volunteers or committee members?*

*4. Has the work been done in a way that meets the stated objective or purpose of the task?*

If these four questions can be answered yes, the work has been done successfully. Whether it has been done according to your own personal work style is not the bottom-line criteria. If you as the leader control too tightly how the volunteers accomplish their tasks, you will wind up creating managers—not thinking, resourceful volunteer leaders.

If any of these four questions is answered no, you and the volunteer need to sit down and evaluate. Perhaps the area of ministry does not fit with the volunteer's gifts, talents, and time schedule. Perhaps the task you have suggested is unrealistic, vaguely defined, or complicated by factors of which you are not aware. Or you may realize that you as the leader have not provided strong enough setup and follow-through for the volunteer. Honestly and openly evaluate and claim whatever responsibility you may have for the volunteer's failure. ◄

► See the Appendix, "Tools for the Leader," page 183, for extra guidelines to help you work with volunteers and leadership teams, including ideas for leading effective meetings and a summary of leadership team-building principles.

► Encourage your volunteer leaders to be part of the evaluation process too. Use Resource 25, "Volunteer Self-Evaluation," page 127, for this purpose.

## BUILDING THE LEADERSHIP TEAM

This chapter has focused on how to enlist and equip volunteers to accomplish the ministry with single adults in your church. It has emphasized the concept that every volunteer is part of your ministry leadership. But as your singles ministry grows, it makes sense to decide at some point to create an ongoing leadership team or leadership "core" to administrate the various programs, events, or activities rather than only using "dream teams." ◄

Drawing the most committed and positive volunteers into a leadership team provides a forum for "visioning," planning, strategizing, and building ministry attitude on an ongoing basis. Team members are experienced volunteers who will accept more responsibility or become trainers or supervisors of other new volunteers.

Chapter 7 identified the "journey of commitment" in a singles ministry and the categories of participants that comprise a singles group. As your singles ministry evolves, it will be important to harness the commitment and leadership of those individuals who most deeply believe and support your outreach for single adults. A leadership team is the ideal gathering point.

Remember that, due to the inflow and outflow of persons involved in your overall singles ministry, you will need to con-

---

## What if Volunteers Fail?[3]

If your leaders fail, ask the following five questions.

1. Did the person understand the job? Was it clear?

2. Was the job appropriate for that person? Did he or she have the necessary skills, experience, or training?

3. Was there someone to help him or her? Or was this person asked to do the job alone? (God does not call us to be Lone Rangers.)

4. Was there a support system of accountability?

5. Did the person feel appreciated and affirmed?

## Team Building Resources

Leadership team building is an art. Specific books written on this topic include:

• *Giving the Ministry Away* by Terry Hershey, Karen Butler, and Rich Hurst. (Elgin, IL: David C. Cook Publishing Co., 1992).

• *Turning Committees into Communities* by Roberta Hestenes. (Colorado Springs: NavPress, 1991).

• *Let Go: A Fresh Look at Effective Leadership in Ministry* by Bobbie Reed and John Westfall. (San Diego, CA: Single Adult Ministry Associates, 1990).

tinually recruit new individuals to add to the leadership team. This helps keep the group open and current, spreads ownership, and enables new leaders to become trained by those more experienced on the team. It also keeps the leadership team alive and strong when attrition occurs.

The regular addition of newcomers to the leadership core helps renew the creativity and vitality of your overall program. New members of the team tend to be the "adventurers," while those who have served much longer often become "settlers." The "adventurers" among you will help keep the ministry's growth pattern alive.

### Good communication is non-negotiable

The emphasis in volunteerism must be placed ultimately upon good communication of what is expected of the volunteer and what the volunteer can expect from the leader. The more open and frequent the communication, the more effective the volunteer work will be.

Remember: *The goal of ministry is not focused on holding events, but upon helping people grow spiritually and relationally.* Enabling and nurturing volunteer involvement provides a channel through which the Holy Spirit can work, challenging and leading single adults to reach toward their God-given potential.

## TOOLS TO HELP YOU

The following worksheet pages are intended to support you and your coworkers as you develop a philosophy and approach to recruiting volunteers. Use them as discussion guides and as launching points for customizing your own unique approach to enlisting and enabling your volunteer leaders.

• **Resource 22, "Volunteer Interest Interview"** *(Guidelines)* Use this form to help each volunteer clarify areas of ministry interest. The volunteer may complete the form alone or as you discuss each question through a personal interview format.

• **Resource 23, "Volunteer Recruitment Worksheet"** *(Sample)* This resource can help you organize your volunteer recruitment intentions and clarify and outline specific job responsibilities and training needs.

• **Resource 24, "Volunteer Ministry Position Description"** *(Worksheet)* Fill out and talk through this form with each volunteer to clarify specific responsibilities. Make two copies—one for the volunteer and one for the singles ministry files for future reference to guide substitutes or new volunteers for the position.

• **Resource 25, "Volunteer Self-Evaluation"** *(Form)* Use this type of form after each event to give volunteers an opportunity to reflect on their service, think through their own standards and goals, and define what the personal and spiritual benefits have been.

# VOLUNTEER INTEREST INTERVIEW

**Name of Volunteer**_____ **Date** _____

**Address**_____ **ZIP** _____

**Phone** *(home)* _____ *(work)* _____

**1. How long have you been part of our singles ministry?** _____

**2. What singles events or activities do you regularly attend at our church?**

**3. Have you participated as a volunteer in our singles ministry or our church before?**
❏ Yes ❏ No   If yes, in what capacity?

**4. What about our singles ministry has been most meaningful or beneficial for you?**

**5. What aspects of our existing singles ministry interest you most?**

*(continued)*

**6. Tell us about yourself.**

- How do you work best? ❐ alone  ❐ as part of a team
- Which describes you best?  ❐ "people oriented"  ❐ "task oriented"
- What skills or special interests do you have?

- How would you like to be more involved in our programs?

- Are there any areas in which you would not like to be involved?  ❐ Yes  ❐ No
  If yes, please list.

**7. Tell us about your availability.**

- What sort of time commitment are you able to make?

- When during the week are you usually available?

- Do you need your "volunteer time" to coincide with the times we offer child care at the church?   ❐ Yes  ❐ No

**8. Optional: Share one or more personal "growing edges" that are central to your life right now.**

Name of interviewer_____ Date_____

# VOLUNTEER RECRUITMENT WORKSHEET

Date_____

Task for which volunteer(s) are needed: _____

Description of volunteer's responsibilities for this task:

Possible volunteers to invite for this task:

| Name | Phone | Date Contacted | Yes | No |
|------|-------|----------------|-----|-----|
|      |       |                |     |     |
|      |       |                |     |     |
|      |       |                |     |     |
|      |       |                |     |     |
|      |       |                |     |     |
|      |       |                |     |     |
|      |       |                |     |     |
|      |       |                |     |     |

**How will the leader or leadership team prepare the volunteer for the task?** *(training session, instructions, meeting, videotape, etc.)*

Other notes:

Recruiter's signature _____ Date _____

# VOLUNTEER MINISTRY POSITION DESCRIPTION

**1. Name of ministry position:** _____

**2. Position description:**




**3. Specific responsibilities for this position:**







**4. Dates or time frame of responsibility:** _____

*(continued)*

**5. Training required:**

**6. Training will be done by:**
❏ Seminar  ❏ Video  ❏ Person _____  ❏ Other_____

**7. Supervisor or staff contact for this volunteer ministry position:**
Name _____ Phone _____
Time and place usually available for contact:_____

**8. Other people who will be working in or with this ministry position:**

| **Name** | **Phone** |
| --- | --- |
| _____ | _____ |
| _____ | _____ |
| _____ | _____ |
| _____ | _____ |
| _____ | _____ |
| _____ | _____ |

**Volunteer's signature** _____ **Date** _____
**Address** _____**ZIP**_____
**Phone** (home) _____ (work) _____

# VOLUNTEER SELF-EVALUATION

Name _____ Phone _____

Name of event/activity _____

Date(s) of event/activity _____

Volunteer position filled _____

**SELF-EVALUATION**

**1. Overall, my experience as volunteer worker/leader was:**
❏ Very Worthwhile   ❏ Adequate   ❏ Not Very Meaningful
**Comments:**

**2. Overall, I would rate my fulfillment of duties as a volunteer or leader of this event as:**
❏ Completed Well   ❏ Adequately Done   ❏ Less Than Adequate
**Comments:**

**3. I arrived early or on time for this event.** ❏ Yes   ❏ No

**4. I was present for all of this event.** ❏ Yes   ❏ No

**5. Something I learned about myself, or a "growing edge" I experienced through being a part of this event, was:**

*(continued)*

6. I would like to lead or volunteer at a similar event again in the future.
❑ Yes  ❑ No
**Comments:**

## EVENT EVALUATION

1. **The meeting room/facilities, media equipment, and availability of sign-in sheets, name tags, etc., were adequate.**  ❑ Yes  ❑ No  **If no, what was missing?**

2. **Some ideas I have for improving this event the next time it may be held are:**

3. **OPTIONAL: People I would recommend for leading/volunteering for a similar event:**

# Money, Money, Money

REPRODUCIBLE RESOURCES AT THE END OF THIS CHAPTER

"No wonder your church has a flourishing singles ministry," one participant told another at a singles conference. "A church your size probably has all the money necessary for a program. But there's no way we could do much for single adults at our church. It's too expensive."

Sound familiar? It's easy to blame a shortage in the church budget for the failure (or absence) of a singles ministry. And it's true that a congregation refusing to budget funds for a singles ministry may signal a dismal lack of support for the whole idea of such a project.

However, those who oversee successful, established singles ministries know a single adult ministry actually can be one of the church's most economical and self-supporting specialty programs. And it brings the church dividends in the form of church growth—more members, more leadership, and ultimately more financial contributions.

---

*"I don't know of any other ministry in the life of the church that can be more cost-effective—from a purely dollars-and-cents perspective—than singles ministry. When someone tells me they can't afford a singles ministry, I tell them they can't afford not to have one."* —BILL FLANAGAN, MINISTER WITH SINGLES AT SAINT ANDREW'S PRESBYTERIAN CHURCH, NEWPORT BEACH, CALIFORNIA[1]

---

If finances seem to be the central struggle for an existing singles ministry, carefully assess the total structure of your program. Are there other reasons the group seems to be floundering? Make sure you're not blaming a small budget for problems actually rooted in poor quality events, lack of organization, unprepared leaders, or other factors. No budget, no matter how large, can remedy such fundamental obstacles.

If you're certain the quality of your singles ministry is consistently good, read on. This chapter will help you realize the importance of cultivating pastoral and congregational support and will give you guidelines to chart your way to fiscal balance. Or if you're just starting a singles group, these suggestions will help you get started on the right foot.

## TWO CRUCIAL INGREDIENTS FOR FINANCIAL SUCCESS

As you develop a budget for your singles ministry, keep in mind that the two most important allies to cultivate are the *senior minister* and the *congregation.* Sound simple? It is simple. It is so simple that some singles groups assume they have this support and don't work to enlist and maintain continued support. ◄

These two ingredients for success are intertwined. Unless the senior minister (and, ideally, the full church staff) leads the way for the congregation to philosophically support the singles program, ministry to and with single adults usually gains little priority, vision, financial backing, or chance for long-term survival. ◄

An example of the significance of these two factors unfolded in a suburban mid-sized church in the southern part of the country. The pastor of this young, growing congregation complained to a consultant that, though he wanted a singles ministry as part of the church programming, he could find no interest or support.

"I know we have many single persons, especially parents, who attend worship services," the pastor shared. "Yet twice we've tried to have a special Sunday morning offering taken as the 'seed money' for a singles group. Both times we received less than twenty dollars!"

As the consultant worked with the pastor to clarify a profile of congregational priorities and pastoral leadership style, a repeated theme emerged. The

► Use the questions on Resource 26, page 136, to establish a clear picture of current and potential financial support for your ministry.

► Communication with your senior pastor is crucial for developing support for the singles ministry vision. Ways to meet and visit with your pastor about singles ministry are described in Chapter 3 on page 53. For more ideas about improving congregational attitudes toward single adult ministry, see Chapter 2, page 36.

pastor frequently preached about the family in traditional terms—husband, wife as homemaker, and children.

Under his guidance, many "traditional family" activities were regularly offered. With his repeated emphasis from the pulpit and through church events designed for the traditional family, the pastor had consistently stressed his own priority of marriage and the nuclear family. He had thus inadvertently trained the congregation to see the traditional family unit as their primary focus.

The pastor began to see how his own area of expertise, helping couples develop strong marriage relationships, had created an unconscious bent to his ministry. He realized he had "set up" the congregation not to be particularly interested in investing in single adults. The pastor admitted he felt uninformed and uncertain about relating to single adult issues and more competent dealing with marriage concerns.

He gained more confidence by studying singles ministry resources and attending a conference on working with singles. With a conscious effort, the pastor made a plan which would help expand both his and his congregation's vision for "the family" in both traditional and nontraditional forms. He learned to use more inclusive sermon illustrations, to include single adults in the worship service, and to offer church events singles would feel comfortable attending.

As the pastor's message of support for single adults became more clear to the congregation, requests for financial backing for the singles ministry received more positive responses. Over time, the congregation followed the pastor's example and leadership. Members began to see single adult ministry as part of the church's mission. The church became more inclusive of single adults and single-parent families.

## SINGLES MINISTRY AND THE CHURCH BUDGET

Does "singles ministry" need to be a line-item in your annual church budget? It's true that a singles ministry can be run successfully by creatively combining a variety of sources for funding. But *legitimacy is given to the singles program in the eyes of the single adults and the congregation if it is part of the church's official budget concerns.* When your singles ministry is listed in the annual church budget, it is established as a priority worthy of financial investment. Singles ministry as a line-item budget entry in the annual church finances directly reflects the church's attitude and priorities concerning a singles program. It often reveals how strongly the congregation views singles ministry as an ongoing part of the church's outreach and its commitment to single adult program growth.

Participants from a large church in the Midwest struggled for several years to start a singles program, but consistently found themselves stuck as a small, struggling support group, unrecognized and unsupported by the congregation. When the single adults finally evaluated their situation, they uncovered some revealing facts. The youth ministry program at their church had a budget in excess of $5,000, a paid youth minister, and a high-quality ministry newsletter which was produced by the church secretaries. The senior pastor promoted the youth program every week from the pulpit, and youth ministry was included in the mission statement of the church.

On the other hand, the singles ministry received $150 annually from the church budget. One of the ministers had been asked to try to find time to help oversee the singles program while maintaining his already full load of pastoral counseling, evangelism, mission outreach, and Christian education programs. The singles newsletter was not prepared by the church office staff, but by whichever single adult had time to do it each month—and it usually looked disorganized and unprofessional. Any money needed beyond the $150 had to be raised by the group itself. The senior pastor seemed to support the singles' activities, but did not promote their events from the pulpit.

This singles group realized their church had not yet developed a commitment to ministry with single adults. They also perceived their existing singles efforts had an "image" problem in the congregation's eyes. They carefully analyzed their current singles program in terms of quality and balance and assessed their present financial needs.

The leaders of the singles group met several times with the senior pastor to discuss the church's interest and support for the singles ministry and its financial needs. Together they began to define methods to improve the congregational attitude toward, and awareness of, single adults.

Finally, along with the pastor, they developed a way to present a request outline for a larger singles budget to the church's finance committee. They substantiated their request by supplying demographics on the growing number of single adults in the church and community plus descriptions of specific needs.

Two years later, they had their own part-time singles ministry staff person, an attractive newsletter executed by the church office, and a good reputation in the community for a quality ministry. Their senior pastor has become an effec-

▶ The procedures of financial self-assessment for your group described here are summarized on Resource 27, "Yearly Financial Planner," page 138.

tive advocate in both the church and community for the benefits of single adult ministry.

Sound complicated? It doesn't have to be—if you proceed with careful thinking, honest assessment, and accurate planning. A singles program of size and depth can operate on a small budget if you and your leadership team develop guidelines to help yourselves and if you work with the pastor and the church to cultivate an attitude of financial support from the congregation.

## How to Begin with Finances

### Survey ways to finance

There are five basic methods of financing your singles ministry. You will probably use a combination of several or all of these methods.

- *Church annual budget line item*
- *Individual donors or special church-wide offering*
- *Fund-raising projects*
- *Registration fees for singles workshops, weeknight classes, or courses (divorce recovery seminars, etc.)*
- *Freewill offerings at singles events*

### Choose what's best for you

What financial arrangements are right for *your* singles group? The following steps can help you and your leadership team make that determination. ◀

*1. Brainstorm with your dream team or leadership team about the realistic amount of money needed for singles ministry activities in the coming months or year.*

---

## Strive to Be Self-Supporting

Well-established singles programs sometimes become so financially self-supporting that they require no general church budget funds at all. If you're just starting your singles ministry, make this your long-range goal. But realize it may be unrealistic to expect your venture to finance itself fully from the start. Remember it fosters congregational support if you do establish financial backing from the church budget to help launch your singles ministry.

What events might you plan? What kinds of funds will they require? Will you need money for child care? Speaker honoraria? Other expenses? Be reasonably detailed in your notes. Then estimate how much of the cost will be covered by registration fees or offerings. Consider any money already in a singles account. This will give you an idea of how much you have and how much you need.

**2. Make a simple, descriptive outline of your proposed ministry program plans, including the projected total amount needed.**

Include in your outline the rationale behind each program or event idea. A simple title of an event with no explanation will not generate support from those outside your singles group as effectively as a well-articulated, brief statement about each program and why you believe it should be part of the ministry to single adults. Also, list the projected amount you believe will be covered by other sources or existing funds.

You are designing this outline to help your leadership team plan and stay on track financially in the coming months. While this outline should not be treated as unalterable or limit your creativity, it will help you target where you think you want the programs to go.

This outline is also ideal to present to the senior minister and the finance committee. It will provide them with a clear, realistic idea of the singles ministry's hopes, goals, and needs.

**3. Cover your bases with the pastor and the finance committee of the church.**

Do not eliminate the senior minister from the "loop" when you are planning the program and finances for your singles activities. The pastor must be kept informed at all times in order to cultivate and maintain support for the singles program. Meet with the pastor and review the outline you have made, asking for sug-

gestions and recommendations. Your pastor can help you with realistic perspective and insight.

If you hope to have the singles ministry become a line item in the church budget, find out how the system works. Churches usually plan budgets on an annual basis. Discover the finance committee's timeline for establishing the budget before each new year begins and submit the completed outline request early.

If at all possible, meet with the finance committee or its chairperson personally to discuss and clarify your plans and financial requests and answer any questions. If you have clearly documented and verified your current and projected financial needs via the outline you have made, you will help the finance committee members make an informed decision as they designate the church budget for the coming year.

Remember: *Unless you ask, you usually will not receive the funding you are seeking.* The members of the finance committee may not be involved in your singles ministry and, therefore, have no idea of the dimensions of your financial needs—or ministry potential—unless they have this outline.

**4. Find out what methods of fund-raising are acceptable (or unacceptable) in your church.**

If you will need to do fund-raising in addition to (or instead of) receiving support from the general church budget, do some homework about the history of fund-raising events at your church. You will discover this information by visiting with the senior pastor. It's also important to find out if certain fund-raising events are traditionally sponsored by other ministries in the church (and therefore are ones your singles group would want to avoid). For example, perhaps the youth group always has a summer car wash, or maybe the women of the church hold an annual crafts bazaar.

Or are some fund-raising techniques incompatible with the philosophical position of the church? For instance, would your congregation or community be offended if you held a "bingo" fundraiser? Understand the parameters and stay within them.

Checking dates with the master church calendar is vital. You will encounter disaster if you try to stage a fund-raiser while another program's fund-raiser in your church is scheduled at or near the same time.

You can raise money in many different ways. However, your leadership team should choose its methods thoughtfully. Consider the group's "image" as you brainstorm fund-raising ideas. If you raise money by projects that might more appropriately fit the youth group (like a car wash), the church will perceive your singles ministry to be filled with over-grown teenagers. If you only host bake sales, your ministry will have an "all women" image. These images may be far from the truth, but they will send signals to the congregation and to singles who may consider attending your program.

Your fund-raising efforts must be adult in nature and easy for a broad range of people to support. Fund-raising for a "common cause" is a good way to unite the your singles ministry participants, as long as it has general appeal and can involve everyone who is available.

### 5. Ask about the feasibility of a special Sunday morning offering.

When you meet with the senior pastor, check on the possibility of a specific offering just for the singles ministry during a Sunday worship service. An occasional offering just for the singles budget serves a dual purpose: providing finances and regularly keeping the singles ministry before the congregation. If this is done on a regular basis (quarterly or even monthly), the church begins to learn responsibility for the singles outreach.

### 6. Explore ways to make your events self-supporting.

Many singles programs fund the bulk (or even all) of their activities by making them self-supporting. If you are holding a divorce recovery workshop, for example, calculate the minimum amount you think you will need to *charge for registration* in order to pay for study materials, child care, and other expenses. If more people register than expected, you will have those additional funds to help pay for your next event. With many classes or courses you can charge a nominal fee to cover expenses or take an offering each time the group meets. If you help people understand the necessity to help under-write the costs, those who can contribute will be motivated to do so.

Instead of charging registration or admission for certain events, consider *taking an offering* at your singles activities. By simply reminding the single adults of the financial needs of the group, some will be encouraged to give to the program. Many single adults give generously to the church. Their giving will be proportional to how important your singles programs are in their lives.

## WORDS TO THE WISE ABOUT MONEY

As you consider how to plan financially for your singles programs, keep in mind the following tips.

### 1. Always seek God's leading.

It's easy to pursue the spectacular, entertaining, or impressive without first considering if it is something God is truly calling your singles ministry to do.

### 2. Always be fiscally responsible with the funds available to your singles ministry.

Your stewardship with the money entrusted to you carries a message to the people in the program and in the congregation. This influences their willingness to make personal contributions or to help with fund-raisers.

For example, one leadership team persuaded the church's financial committee to budget $1000 for a large singles event. They planned carefully and were successful making the event fully self-supporting by charging a registration fee. The leadership team then decided to use the budgeted money to give themselves each a full scholarship to a regional singles conference, including renting a vehicle and covering all meal expenses.

They did not reveal this use of the funds until after the conference, when they were asking for money in the next year's church budget. Naturally, they were frustrated when no money was granted them for the next year. Why? They had not been accountable in decision-making for the use of the funds. The congregation and singles group felt the leadership's agenda had been self-serving. Had the leadership team made the scholarship decision with the full knowledge of the group and even the church's finance committee, they might have won favorable support.

**3. Don't exhaust the congregation or your singles group by constantly complaining about a lack of money.**

Constant complaining about money sends signals that you think your singles ministry is failing! Again, evaluate your singles activities and make sure you're not blaming a lack of quality, poor organization, or ineffective leadership skills on a small budget.

Lack of financial support is often a sign that the senior pastor, church members, or singles themselves do not see the singles outreach as a valuable investment. Work to make your events high quality and to help educate others about the worth of singles ministry and the opportunities you have to reach out to new people in the community. People usually give generously when they understand the need and necessity of the ministry.

---

*"People are much inclined to believe what they read. Often, they read more into it than the writer intended. Contrary to what some church treasurers and finance committee members think, not everyone responds to negative financial reports with generous gifts to 'help us catch up.' Some people see negative figures as proof that they have been making a bad investment."* —HERB MILLER[2]

---

## TOOLS TO HELP YOU

The reproducible resources on the following pages can help you and your leadership team plan the financial future of your program. May your decisions be characterized by vision, realism, and good stewardship as God leads you.

• **Resource 26, "Financial Support Evaluation" (Discussion Guide)** Use this discussion guide to help you and your leadership team establish a clear picture of how you need to develop needed support for your ministry.

• **Resource 27, "Yearly Financial Planner" (Worksheet)** Use this worksheet to estimate a total yearly budget. List the events you plan to have during the coming calendar year. Estimate the cost of each event, think through how much money might be generated or gained (by registration fees, freewill offerings, or other sources) and how much additional money might be needed during each month. Your completed chart will help you when appealing to the finance committee for support.

# FINANCIAL SUPPORT EVALUATION

## CONGREGATIONAL SUPPORT

1. What seems to be our congregation's current commitment level to our singles ministry?

2. What evidence do we have to support our conclusions?

3. What would it take to improve congregational support?

## PASTORAL SUPPORT

What kind of support does our singles ministry (or our plan to start a singles ministry) have from our senior pastor?

*NOTE: If you have not met with the senior pastor, make an appointment to discuss your plans and to ask a few questions, including the following ones.*

*1. Pastor, do you see the congregation as supportive and open to developing a single adult ministry? Explain.*

*2. In what ways could the singles ministry be promoted throughout the Christian education program and worship services?*

*(continued)*

3. *Is it possible to gain church budget support for a singles ministry? If yes, what route should be taken to pursue this?*

## FINANCIAL SUPPORT

1. Is our singles program part of the all-church annual budget? ❏ Yes ❏ No  Why?

2. If our singles program is not a part of the all-church annual budget, what route can we take to pursue that possibility? *(If you're not sure, ask the senior pastor or chairperson of the church finance committee.)*

3. What are some available financial resources for underwriting some or all of our activities? *(List them and discuss the feasibility of each.)*

4. What could we try as a fund-raising project to help underwrite our singles group or programs this year? *(Brainstorm ideas, then eliminate any which are not "age" and "image" appropriate.)*

# YEARLY FINANCIAL PLANNER
## YEAR _____

| MONTH | PROJECTED EVENTS | Cost of Event | Income from Event | BALANCE NEEDED |
|---|---|---|---|---|
| January | | | | |
| February | | | | |
| March | | | | |
| April | | | | |
| May | | | | |
| June | | | | |
| July | | | | |
| August | | | | |
| September | | | | |
| October | | | | |
| November | | | | |
| December | | | | |
| **TOTAL ESTIMATE OF MONEY NEEDED FOR THE YEAR:** *(Add up amounts in last column.)* | | | | $ |

# Promoting and Publicizing Your Singles Ministry

REPRODUCIBLE RESOURCES AT THE END OF THIS CHAPTER

The best promotion for your singles ministry begins through offering a quality program. Begin all your promotional efforts by making sure you can be proud of the program and believe it will minister to the needs of single adults. Quality activities are a pleasure to promote and will build your church's reputation with the singles population of your community.

No matter how much time or money your singles ministry invests in advertising, the most effective means of promotion (negative or positive) will be through what those who attend your events tell their single friends. Make sure every event you sponsor is based on thoughtful planning and thorough preparation. ◄

Promoting your singles ministry through advertising, newsletters, flyers, posters, or handouts is your secondary means of letting people know your program has something important for them. A person who has never attended your ministry will judge what your group is like by the appearance of your promotional material. All publicity must clearly, simply, and professionally convey the image and the value of your program. Publicity can be a great asset or a great handicap to your program, so make sure it is quality.

> ► For every event you plan, use a copy of Resource 28, "Promotion & Publicity," page 150, to summarize the important details of promotion and publicity.

---

*"I'm convinced that if you're interested in fulfilling the Great Commission, the use of advertising media is a must."*
—RICH KRALJEV, SINGLES MINISTER[1]

---

## BASICS OF PROMOTIONAL MATERIAL

Publicity pieces need not be large, flashy, or multi-colored. They do not have to be created by a graphic designer and printed on a laser printer. However, your publicity literature must be clear, concise, and correct. It must include enough details so a new person can easily understand how to attend and what to expect.

Even if a promotional piece conveys useful information, those receiving it will be distracted if it contains misspelled words, poor grammar, or misplaced punctuation. The information must be organized in a logical and easily-understood layout. A shoddy publicity piece will make the reader think your group is haphazard, careless, disorganized, or illiterate. *Never distribute any publicity piece until it has been proofread by at least one other person (preferably two).* Set your quality standards high and stick to them.

When you compile the information for your publicity, include all the basics.

### 1. Who is sponsoring the event?

Give not only the name of your singles group, but also the name of your church. If your group's name includes initials or abbreviations, state what they stand for. For example, "First Church S.A.M." means nothing to many people unless you note that S.A.M. stands for Single Adult Ministry.

### 2. When and where will the event be held?

Specify whether you mean "7:30 A.M." or "7:30 P.M." Also indicate the day, date, and exact location (include directions if it is hard to find). If the group meets in your church, list the room number or name; also note which church door to enter. Newcomers will be disgruntled if they encounter five different entrances and have no idea where to find the "church parlor." If parking is a challenge, include directions on where to park.

### 3. What is the event?

A catchy name for an event doesn't always reveal what the event will be. If it's a Bible study, party, support group, or educational event, say so.

### 4. Who is invited to the event?

This is one of the most pressing questions single adults have when reading promotional literature. If the promotional material is not clear about the intended audience of the event, newcomers will probably choose not to attend. Is it only for single parents? Is it targeted for young adults? Older adults? All ages?

### 5. Is a cost involved?

If participants will be expected to buy a study book, include the cost of the book in the promotional material. If the event has a registration fee or if an offering will be taken, mention this in the publicity. Participants want to know what to expect.

### 6. Will child care be available?

If you provide child care, parents need to know if there is a cost, what ages of children will be accepted, and where the child-care room is located.

### 7. How can participants preregister, if required?

Clearly state to whom the check should be made payable and the address to which it should be sent. If you have a preregistration deadline, state the date (and time of day) of the deadline in bold letters.

### 8. Who can be called for more information?

Even if you've included all necessary information in your publicity, some people may still want to call a contact person for more details. Therefore, include the name and phone number of a contact person who will be available to receive calls. Nothing is more frustrating for new people than to repeatedly call a contact person who is never available or who doesn't return phone messages.

### PREPARING PROMOTIONAL MATERIAL

Your publicity flyers, newsletters, brochures, and posters must look clear, clean, organized, and as professional as possible. Some churches have a member of the support staff with computer skills who can produce wonderful materials. You may or may not have this luxury at your disposal. If not, your publicity can still look good even though produced by individuals who are not desktop publishing experts. Attention to quality and detail will lead you down the right paths. (Even if a computer isn't available, using a typewriter with a new ribbon—plus a little creativity—works.)

Think about how to organize the information attractively on the page. "Clip art" (small pieces of artwork, cartoons, designs, or borders) is a popular way to add interest to your publicity pieces, but don't overdo it. Remember: The image you create with the clip art will be the image readers have of your group. Too much clip art (or the wrong clip art) can look unprofessional or juvenile.

---

## Good Publicity Requires Teamwork

If you are a staff person who oversees the singles ministry at your church, it is best if you do not assume total responsibility for the promotional work. Gather a team of laypeople and share accountability for creating good publicity.

"Please avoid the mistake that many churches make: assigning the marketing leadership role to the pastor. This assignment should not automatically be given to the pastor. Even in a church where things happen almost exclusively as a result of the pastor's strength of character and will, a marketing plan may not receive the attention and consideration it needs from someone who is already bogged down in daily church operations." —George Barna[2]

*Try to let your promotional material be created by a team of people, rather than by only one person.* Often in a singles ministry there is an individual who has professional expertise or a strong interest in this area. It's easy to let this one person take charge and develop such ownership of the publicity that it becomes difficult to suggest changes or improvements.

The best publicity is created by a team of two or three people who can brainstorm, offer each other suggestions, then carefully proofread each other's work for accuracy, completeness, spelling, and punctuation. This spreads the ownership and responsibility to more people, lessening the likelihood of burnout. This team should perpetually train new people to become part of the publicity team. Then when some team members retire, new members are ready to carry on the work.

## TIPS ON CREATING A PROFESSIONAL LOOK

According to Robert Simerly in *Planning and Marketing Conferences and Workshops*,[3] there are several crucial elements to remember when creating visual effects on posters, flyers, brochures, and newsletters.

### 1. Design your promotional materials according to your audience.

The layout must be bold enough to draw the viewer's attention within three to five seconds. It must also elicit the right "feel" from the targeted audience. Do not use ultra-contemporary graphics and copy for a traditional audience or a traditional look for a younger, more contemporary audience.

### 2. In general, try to use only two or three different typefaces or fonts (letter styles) within the same promotional piece.

Different typefaces can be used for emphasis or to command attention, but continuity of typeface throughout most of the material makes it easier to read and provides a more professional look. Use a typeface size that is easily readable by all ages. A common error, especially in newsletters, is using a typeface size that's so small it frustrates people who wear bifocals. It is better to cut down the length of your information in order to allow larger print.

### 3. Choose dark blue or black ink.

Dark blue and black ink are the easiest colors to read. (Red is the hardest to read.) According to studies done on what attracts readers' attention, using more than one color of ink on promotional pieces does not necessarily enhance readership response. It is more expensive to use multiple colors—but if you have the capability to do so, use second or third colors only to highlight or accent.

### 4. If using photographs, make sure they are of professional (or near professional) caliber and portray the subject favorably.

Even if your promotional piece is well written, it will not succeed if the snapshots included are blurred and fail to present a positive image of your singles ministry. Rather than having dark, blurry, or poorly composed photos, it is better to use no photos. Also, if you use action shots of people who attend your programs, be sure they are representative of the promotional piece's target audience. For example, do not picture older adults in a flyer for the "twentysomething" crowd. Or don't use a photo containing all women when you hope to attract both men and women to your event.

### 5. Choose paper color to allow maximum readability.

White or ivory paper allows the easiest reading. If you choose other paper colors, make sure the contrast between the ink and paper colors is adequate. For example, using medium green ink on red paper would cause people to struggle when trying to read your publication.

## METHODS OF PROMOTION

You and your leadership should brainstorm every conceivable way to publicize your singles program—the sky is the limit! After making your list, discern which channels of communication are most effective in your community. Does the singles population in your city have a favorite radio station they listen to, or do they prefer to read the newspaper? Would a poster in the town's grocery store and flyers at the cash register target most of the local population? Or would a special mailing to your community be more effective? When you've decided which methods are best for your location, use them as the primary tools to let people know about your programs.

As you brainstorm, consider the following possible means of publicizing events.

### 1. Publicize over the phone

Depending on the size of your community, the size of your singles group, and the state of development of your singles ministry, phone calling can be a simple and effective means of promoting events. *Phone calling is especially crucial to a newly-forming singles group, in which personal contact and personal invitation is essential.*

For example, the members of the leadership team in one singles group each pledged to call and invite three friends to the next event. Since there were four on the leadership team, twelve people were contacted who might not have attended without a personal invitation. Inviting someone personally over the phone may be just the impetus he or she needs to try the group.

Some smaller singles groups have "phone trees" to alert members of activity schedules. (A "phone tree" is a calling list that has been distributed to all regular participants. The first person on the list calls two people; each of those people calls two more people, and so on.) Remember that though this works well for those already participating in your ministry, it may not be the best method for reaching new people. ▶

### 2. Publicize through the mail

Many singles programs develop a monthly *singles newsletter*. Creating a regular newsletter can help you build a mailing list of individuals interested in the singles ministry. At the same time, it gives you a way to reach them with information on a regular basis.

Plan your newsletter format thoughtfully. It does not have to be spectacular, showy, ornate, or overdone. Nor should it be subdued, dull, or lifeless!

*Overall purpose and tone.* The purposes of the newsletter are to inform attenders about activities and to give new people a glimpse of your singles ministry. Carefully choose the tone of your newsletter. Let it portray your singles ministry as an upbeat, quality, positive singles outreach aimed at people who want to grow and lead healthy life-styles. A "poor, lonely singles" image conveyed by the newsletter will be a definite detriment to the growth potential of your group.

*Specific goals.* With your planning or leadership team, develop a short list of goals for your newsletter. Is it only to inform readers about events? Should it also be devotional or inspirational? Should it help readers get acquainted with the pastor, ministry, staff, and others? Is it a tool to communicate your goals for the singles ministry? Is it primarily intended to reach potential attenders? Is it a combination of these—and more? Be clear about what you hope the newsletter will accomplish and do a self-

◀ Chapter 6, "All about Follow-Up," includes information on using phone follow-up with visitors to your singles events. See Resource 18, "What to Say on the Phone," page 96, for suggestions on using the phone to follow-up and invite new people.

check each month before mailing it to be sure it lines up with your stated goals.

For example, if you want your newsletter to appeal to to the regular attender, the "sometimes" attender, as well as the newcomer, read the copy from all three perspectives and edit it accordingly.

If you send your newsletter to people who request information about your singles ministry, make sure it does not include "inside" jokes or assumptions that the readers will automatically know the last names of the contact people and how to reach them.

*Details, details, details.* The same basic criteria used in writing other promotional material also applies to the information placed in your newsletter. Include all details for each event so even a new person reading your newsletter can easily attend any activity described.

Nothing alienates a potential attender more than reading a newsletter that raises more questions than it answers. (The following examples were found in real newsletters; only the names have been changed to protect the guilty!)

*Call Joe if you have questions.*
*(Who is Joe? What is his phone number? When can he be reached?)*

*Remember Nancy's driving and John's choice of dinner menu from last month? Our next Lunch Bunch will meet at the church next Sunday at our usual time for eating out together and another hilarious occasion.*

*(Who is invited to the "Lunch Bunch"? When is "the usual time"? Where will the group eat? Are children welcome? Do those references to Nancy and John mean this group is already a clique and would feel closed to newcomers?)*

*Dear friends,*
*Thank you for all the hard work you've done with our Breakfast Club. It's been a great program, and I've been so proud of you all. If you've never been to the Breakfast Club, I invite you to attend and meet a lot of wonderful people.*
*Sincerely, Jane*

*(This letter appeared on the front page of a singles newsletter. What is the Breakfast Club? Who is it for? When is it held? What does it cost? Who is Jane—a staff person or the program chairperson? How can a person find out more?)*

*Here are the dates and times for our groups this month. Mark your calendars now!*
*D.R.W.—Sept. 12 at 7:00 P.M.*
*Y.A.M.—Sundays at 6:00 P.M.*
*P.H.D.—Sept. 24 at 7:30 P.M.*
*S.A.M. Core—Sept. 29 at 6:30 P.M.*

---

## Guidelines for Writing Publicity

In *Putting Your Best Foot Forward*, Steve Diggs, promotional expert, offers these simple guidelines when writing publicity or newsletters:

- *Get right to the point.* Don't waste the reader's time.
- *Remain focused.* Don't let your copy wander in an extraneous direction.
- *Avoid stale, trite words and phrases.*
- *Don't make grand promises that threaten your credibility.* Words like "best," "most," "biggest," "wonderful," and "new" are worn out. Over the years, they've lost their punch. Use them selectively.
- *Use high-impact words.* Examples include "now," "yes," "no," "fight," "love," "hate," "happy," "worry," and "today."
- *Never say with ten words what can be said with five words.*[4]

---

## More Tips on Newsletters

**Your newsletter does not have to be lengthy.** Do not include "filler" articles just to increase its size. It is also not meant to be a "gossip chain," or a place to highlight couples who got married that month. If your singles ministry is based on an attitude that the single life-style is normal and acceptable, your newsletter should reflect that philosophy. Keep away from appearing to hint in your newsletter that those who have achieved marriage have "finally succeeded" and have "graduated into full adulthood."

---

*(What are these groups? Who are they for? What do all those initials stand for? Where do they meet?)*

*Content and layout.* As mentioned, a well-done newsletter contains basic information to tell people about your singles ministry and its purpose. The front page should feature description and details about an exciting upcoming event, rather than a report about a past activity. This draws the readers immediately into what your singles ministry has to offer, rather than letting them know what they have missed.

Some established singles ministries feature a monthly column or letter by the singles minister, singles staff worker, or the chairperson of the singles leadership team. If the same person always writes such a feature, the readers may feel the entire ministry revolves around that one person. If you choose to have a letter or regular article which is inspirational in nature, consider rotating that responsibility among your leadership.

Many newsletters include a "calendar page" listing the month's schedule of events. If you use abbreviations or initials in the small calendar squares, define them elsewhere on the same page for easy reference.

### 3. Publicize at events

Always have newsletters, flyers, or brochures publicizing upcoming events at each event you hold. Also include items such as your printed purpose statement, an information page about singles classes on Sunday mornings, a brochure describing the various fellowship and support groups, and literature about your church in general—including Sunday service times. This is a key promotional opportunity for helping people find ways to become more involved with your singles ministry and congregation as a whole.

In preparing simple flyers or brochures for this purpose, follow the same basic rules of any good publicity. Include all pertinent information, arranged in a visually-appealing way. Eliminate spelling, grammatical, or punc-

---

## Naming Your Newsletter

**If you title your singles ministry newsletter, focus on clarity and communication when choosing the name.** Acronyms are generally poor newsletter names because your audience may not understand what the initials mean. Even though your newsletter will be mailed to a population of single persons, your title should clearly indicate that the publication features programs for singles. Let the title tell the tale.

**"Bear in mind that you wish those seeing your newsletter for the first time to become interested enough to at least begin reading it.** That means, usually, that the title of the newsletter must 'grab' them at once, preferably by appealing immediately to their direct interests." —Herman Holtz[5]

---

tuation errors. Always include your church's name, full mailing address, and phone number with area code on each piece of literature you produce. Never distribute flyers with incorrect or outdated information.

If you have an information table at your events, invite well-informed group members to be available for answering questions.

### 4. Publicizing throughout the church

When submitting articles on your events for publication in the Sunday bulletin or all-church newsletter, be thorough with details. Also, always get your articles to the church office on or before the deadline. This will make a good impression on behalf of the singles ministry.

Place flyers about your singles ministry in the church foyer and church office (and wherever people gather), especially on Sunday mornings. Talk to your pastor about announcing important singles events from the pulpit.

Other churches in your community who do not have singles groups may want to give their single adults information about your events. Consider delivering or mailing materials about your events to other local churches. Include a friendly letter to the pastor, explaining your intention to provide fellowship and growth for single adults in the area, along with the name and phone number of a contact person. Other churches may decide to include information about your events in their announcements or church bulletins, providing they are not in conflict with the regular schedule at their church.

### 5. Publicizing in the community

*Good publicity methods.* To promote the singles ministry in your community, brainstorm every possible method. For example, paid advertising or public service announcements on the radio or in the newspaper; free cable television channel time; classified ads in the newspaper; posters in laundromats, apartment building lobbies, health clubs, libraries, doctors' offices, grocery or other stores; letters to divorce attorneys, counselors, therapists, and social service agencies who have single adults as clients. Some singles ministries use a banner across the front of the church or a billboard on the church lawn for pedestrians or drivers to see as they pass.

Try to think creatively where to place publicity so the most people will see it. If you're targeting Christians, place your newspaper advertisement on the religion page. If you're targeting the unchurched, try the entertainment and movie page, the editorial page, the sports section, or even the personal ads section.

Good publicity can be done with a low budget. If buying a newspaper or radio advertisement is beyond your group's financial means, however, invest some time and energy in posting and distributing promotional literature at key locations around town.

Public service announcements are usually published free of charge in newspapers and announced without cost on most radio stations.

If you are uncertain how to write a public service announcement for the radio or newspaper, follow the sample on page 147, or call and ask the appropriate person at the radio station or office. Explaining your event may capture media interest and even precipitate the radio or newspaper's pursuit of a story about your activities. This is some of the best free advertising of all!

Again, make all your promotional contacts as high quality as possible. They reflect on your ministry. The importance of your audience must be reflected in the caliber of your promotional materials.

Remember: *Publicity pieces do not have to be sophisticated, but they must be high* quality and include all of the necessary information. ▶

**Poor publicity methods.** At the end of a recent event held by an established singles ministry, the "emcee" asked if anyone in the group had any special announcements. Several responded: someone from the single parents' support group announced a picnic; a representative from the young adults' fellowship group gave the date and time of a young adult outing. These were "in house" announcements about other programs within the singles ministry of that church.

Then someone else stood up. "I'm representing another congregation," he said. "We're trying to start a singles group at our church. We're having the first event next week, and I'd like to invite everyone here to come. I've brought flyers for everyone." He quickly passed the flyers down each row.

This actual incident illustrates two cautions regarding publicity methods.

**1. Don't give an open invitation, allowing anyone who who wishes to make an announcement.** Otherwise you risk two things: (a) having someone give an announcement that is counter to your church or ministry's philosophy or purpose or (b) having someone with a legitimate announcement to make miss an important detail because he or she was not prepared.

In your singles ministry, establish a policy that anyone with an announcement to make should clear it with you first. This gives you the opportunity to evaluate whether or not the announcement is appropriate and to make sure the announcer has all the details well in mind. Ideally, people making announcements

◀ For samples of quality singles ministry publicity pieces that simply and easily (anyone could do them), see Resources 29-32, pages 152-155.

---

## Sample Public Service Announcement Letter

May 2, 1994

Religion Editor
Journal/Star
500 State Street
Anytown, Anystate 33333

Dear Editor,

Would you please include the following information in your "Religion Notes" column on Saturday, May 14? Thank you for helping us spread the word about this important upcoming event for the single adults in our city and surrounding communities.

> First Church (320 Main Street) will hold its monthly "Singles Forum" for single adults of all ages this Sunday, May 15 from 7:00 to 8:30 P.M. in Fellowship Hall. Jill Jeffries, personnel trainer at United Corporation, will offer a program called, "Personality Types: Understanding Ourselves and Others." Pre-registration is not required. A freewill offering will be taken during the evening. Free child care will be available during the presentation.

We appreciate your support with this publicity!

Please contact me at _____ for more information.

Sincerely,

should read it from a prepared statement of details or at least refer to a cue card.

**2. Don't try to steal someone else's sheep.** True, all singles ministries should see themselves as a team, working together to reach every single adult in the area. But each singles group has its own unique mission and circle of influence or impact. Simply attending another established singles ministry and trying to recruit its membership does not help reach the unchurched single adults in the community. And it's not a good place to publicize without permission!

If you are starting a new singles group, do not put flyers on the cars at another church's singles event. Do not try to recruit those who have already found purpose in an existing program. Work within the boundaries of your own church and organization. Reach new people whom you've targeted as still needing what you have to offer. Others may leave their singles groups and attend yours by their own decision. Welcome them! But remain a team player with other singles programs and respect their work and efforts.

You may wish at some point to plan a cooperative event with another church's singles group. This is a good way to establish a teamwork relationship with them. But be sensitive and considerate to their ministry, as you would like them to be sensitive to yours.

## FINAL TIPS ON PUBLICITY

### Check your publicity effectiveness

How can you evaluate the effectiveness of your publicity and promotional efforts? Routinely ask regular attenders if, and where, they have seen your publicity. Casually ask newcomers how they found out about your programs. Listen carefully to the answers you receive. They will probably reveal the most effective means of getting your information to people.

You will probably find that word-of-mouth is one of the most powerful publicity routes. Remember that the attenders of your singles ministry hold an important key to the program's growth by inviting their friends to come. Remind them to do so!

---

*"The word of mouth process takes time. It does not generate large crowds at first. What it does generate is superior retention. People who come to your group through personal referral are far more likely to stay than those attracted by other forms of advertising."*

—JOHN ETCHETO[6]

---

### Get others to help

You may be thinking, I can't do it all! Publicity takes too much work for me to cover it! Hopefully you do feel this way—because effective promotion should not be done by just one person. The more people involved in the area of promotion, the more chance you have for successful outreach. Your job is to spread the involvement and ownership to the most people possible.

What happens if you feel you can't find enough people to help with publicity? Ask yourself these serious questions:

- *Is it important to me only, or is it also important to the group?*
- *If it's important to the group, why aren't others volunteering to help with it?*

One possible answer might have to do with *how* you are inviting people to help with promotion. Review Chapter 8 about building and nurturing leadership and how to recruit volunteers.

Another possibility might be that you are blocking people from feeling the need to help with publicity, because you are trying to do it all yourself. Ask God to show you how to get out of the way so He can work in the lives of the people, empowering them to do the work of the ministry together.

**Do All to the Glory of God**

The results of successful promotion and publicity can be truly rewarding. Remember to glorify God's name and purpose in all that you do as you represent your group to the community, town, or city. Good publicity imparts the vision of your singles ministry to others in an exciting and inviting way. Let nothing stop you from giving your best effort to the task.

## TOOLS TO HELP YOU

• **Resource 28, "Promotion & Publicity"** *(Worksheet)* For every event you plan, use a copy of this worksheet to summarize the important details that need to be taken care of and communicated.

• **Resources 29-32—"Singles on Sunday," "There is Life After Divorce," "Single Parents Seminar," and "Fourth of July Potluck Picnic"** *(Promotional Samples)* These samples of actual publicity pieces were inexpensive and easy to produce. They illustrate clear and simple communication, yet have a professional look anyone can achieve.

# PROMOTION & PUBLICITY

Event name _____ Date _____ Time _____ to _____

## GENERAL INFORMATION

1. Description of the event:


2. Exact Location:


3. Special directions to find location:


4. Target audience: *(people invited)* _____

5. Fees: *(if any)*   Registration $ _____ Child care fee $ _____ Other $ _____

6. Child care specifics:


7. Preregistration procedures and deadline: *(if any)*


## CONTACT PERSON

1. Name _____ Phone _____
2. Availability *(What time of day should people call?):* _____

*(continued)*

## PUBLICITY STRATEGY

1. Publicity Committee Members                                    Phone

_____     _____

_____     _____

_____     _____

_____     _____

2. Deadline for completing promotional materials: _____

3. Proofreader(s) of promotional materials:

**Names**                                                    **Phone**

_____     _____

_____     _____

**4. Publicity Schedule:** *(List the destination [newspaper, radio station, Sunday school class, store, etc.], means [phone call, mailing, poster, verbal announcement, etc.], and date to be completed. When task is done, check the box in the last column.)*

| **Destination** | **Means** | **Date** | **Done** |
|---|---|---|---|
| 1. _____ | _____ | _____ | ☐ |
| 2. _____ | _____ | _____ | ☐ |
| 3. _____ | _____ | _____ | ☐ |
| 4. _____ | _____ | _____ | ☐ |
| 5. _____ | _____ | _____ | ☐ |

## MISCELLANEOUS NOTES

☐ **YES, a copy of this promotional material was placed in the "publicity file" of our singles ministry for future reference.**

**This worksheet was completed by** _____

**Date** _____

## Welcome to First Church's . . .

# *"Singles on Sundays"*

### Sunday Schedule for Single Adults of All Ages:

9:45–10:00 A.M.:     Coffee, doughnuts, and conversation in Fellowship Hall.

10:00–11:00 A.M.:     All singles meet together in Upper Youth Hall. We'll have announcements and introductions, then break into mini-classes. New classes will begin each six weeks. Choose the group which interests you most!

### Fall Classes beginning September 11:

<u>Living Responsibly in an Age of Excuses</u>—This class is based upon an intriguing book by Kurt Bruner. What roles does our Christian faith play in the daily choices we make about work, friends, family, and other interests? How can we tell when we've used God's wisdom in creating a responsible life-style for ourselves? Paula Babbitt is the class leader.

<u>That's What the Man Said</u>—The timeless truths of Scripture can make a transforming impact on our daily lives. Each week a different leader will share an inspirational look at how the words of Jesus relate to our decisions, our perspectives, and our futures. This class is based on Maxie Dunnam's popular book by the the same title.

<u>Untwisting Twisted Relationships</u>—Our lives are a complicated pattern of relationships with family members, coworkers, friends, and significant others. Is it possible to bring balance and clarity to these relationships to make them healthy? According to this book by Christian counselor William Backus, the answer is "Yes!" Class leader is Dave Schoneweis.

11:15 A.M.:     Sunday worship service in the sanctuary. Many singles sit together—we invite you to join us for church as we leave Upper Youth Hall after classes!

• First Church Singles Ministry•
• 20th and State Streets • Anytown, Anystate 33333 • (123) 555-7890•

# THERE IS LIFE AFTER DIVORCE

That's what First Church believes. And so this winter we're again offering our Divorce Recovery Workshop—a six-week, Saturday night event designed to help persons move through the tragedy of a failed marriage or broken relationship and gain a new start toward health and wholeness.

It's true: Many people extend the time of their personal recovery from divorce because they don't know of or aren't willing to appropriate the resources available for growth. This workshop is designed to help participants work through their present crisis as quickly and productively as possible. We believe there *is* life after divorce—and, though healing takes time and effort, we can help you find the tools needed to begin the journey.

The workshop will meet for six consecutive Saturday evenings January 16 through February 20 from 7:00–9:00 P.M. in the church Fellowship Hall. Nancy Fly, instructor at Union College, will be the workshop presenter. The program format contains both presentation of information and time in discussion groups, all within a caring and confidential context and Christian perspective. A special bonus of the workshop will include an optional seventh-week session featuring question-and-answer time with both a divorce attorney and a child counselor who specializes in the effects of divorce on children.

Registration cost is $20, which covers course materials, refreshments, and child care, if needed. (Please enter the church by the south double doors. Fellowship Hall is at the top of the stairs.)

Do you know of a friend, relative, or coworker who might benefit from this event? Please pass this information on—or call the Singles Ministry at 123-555-7890 for additional registration forms. Early registration is encouraged.

---

✂

Name_____   Phone_____

Address_____   ZIP _____

**Divorce Recovery Workshop**
January 16–February 20, 1994
(Saturday evenings) 7:00–9:00 P.M.

❑ Registration fee of $20 enclosed.
❑ Yes, I will need child care. Number and ages of children_____

**Mail to:**   **First Church Singles Ministry (phone 123-555-7890)**
**320 Main Street**
**Anytown, Anystate 33333**

# DI♥ORCE RECOVERY WORKSHOP

# Single Parents Seminar

**First Church, 320 Main, Anytown, Anystate 33333**

### June 9–July 14, 7:00–8:30 P.M.
(Wednesday evenings—Church Parlor)
**Cost $10** (includes resource materials and child care if needed)

Are you a single parent (custodial or noncustodial) who struggles to survive the challenge of a single-parent family? Are you newly single, and wondering how to escape falling into the "super-parent" trap, yet do an effective job with your children and your own life priorities? Do you feel alone as a single parent, and would you like to meet others who share a similar experience?

The new First Church "Single Parents Seminar" is a six-week event geared to help single parents meet their challenges successfully—how to be a competent parent, and how to build a healthy family life no matter how diverse the circumstances. Resource for this seminar is *The Fresh Start Single Parenting Workbook* by Thomas Whiteman, which will be provided for each participant. Whatever your situation, this material lets you apply the information to our own setting. The seminar will be led by Jane Doe, a single parent and member of First Church. The format of each week's session will include a step-by-step look at the key aspects of single-parent life, plus time for sharing and support.

If you have further questions, please call the Singles Ministry at 123-555-7890. (Limited scholarship help is available.)

Please enter the church by the west door. The church parlor is located directly to the left as you enter the building.

✂ ·······································································································································································

Name_____   Phone_____

Address_____   ZIP _____

### Single Parents Seminar
June 9–July 14, 7:00-8:30 P.M.
(Wednesday evenings—Church Parlor)

❑ Registration fee of $10 enclosed.
❑ Yes, I will need child care. Number and ages of children _____

**Mail to:   First Church Singles Ministry
Single Parents Seminar
320 Main Street
Anytown, Anystate 33333   (Phone 123-555-7890)**

# Especially for Small Churches

REPRODUCIBLE RESOURCES AT THE END OF THIS CHAPTER

Every church can minister to single adults, but can every church have a singles ministry program? Adult singles in small churches often have a misconception that singles ministry can only succeed in a large city or sizable congregation. Such mentality about what qualifies as "successful ministry" needs to be changed.

Reality says a small church will not have the same numerical base of participants as a large church, but a smaller constituency does not eliminate the need for ministry with single adults.

## DISTINCT CHARACTERISTICS OF SMALL-CHURCH SINGLES GROUPS

### Methodology

Not every effective large-church singles program works in a small church, because the small-membership church is uniquely different—in its concept of ministry, overall program design and emphasis, congregational personality, degree of volunteerism, and general church administration. A small church is not just a scaled-down version of a large church!

Generally speaking, ministry for and with single adults in the small church must include a clear appreciation for the distinct characteristics of small-church methodology. For example, divorce recovery ministry in a large church might take the shape of 100 people gathered in the fellowship hall, listening to a speaker talk about how to survive a failed relationship. Divorce recovery in the small church might consist of three people in the living room of a church member's home, watching a videotape on divorce recovery, followed by sharing, discussion, and prayer together. Both settings can offer a viable ministry of healing. This illustrates what it means to adapt your ministry methods to your own church type, community size, and resources.

### Rural, urban, and metropolitan profiles

What is the definition of a small church? According to Anthony Pappas, author of *Entering the World of the Small Church* (and small-church pastor for eighteen years), a small church usually means a congregation with under 100 members, or with attendance of less than 125 at Sunday worship. In a small church, people know (or expect to know) everyone in the church. When the membership or attendance grows to the point that it is no longer possible to be acquainted with everyone (usually beyond 200), the dynamics of the congregation change and the church no longer fits the "small church" definition.

Pappas suggests four distinct small church "personalities." Rural and urban small churches share similar profiles. A small church in a small rural community has a close-knit congregation where everyone knows everyone. Similarly, a small church in an urban setting displays the same close-knit traits because its neighborhood takes on the same characteristics as a small town—where there is a family feel and everybody is acquainted.

The metropolitan small church is different in some significant ways. A small metropolitan church is one that incorpo-

---

## Don't Apologize . . . Celebrate Your Ministry

**If you are planning (or already have) a singles group in your small church, don't ever apologize for what you are doing for single adults!** Wonderful things can happen in small groups. Your singles ministry is not discredited just because you don't have the higher-profile events that a larger budget or bigger membership allows. Don't compare yourselves to other singles ministries. Celebrate the community of single adults God has drawn together at your church. Continually strive to minister to one another and to reach out to others.

rates attenders from all over the city, thus avoiding the neighborhood or small-town interconnectedness which is typical in rural and urban small churches.

The suburban small church is a congregation that may have begun as a rural church, but the city has gradually crept out and surrounded it. If so, a positive suburban small church may still retain its rural-type sense of identity and importance as a vital part of the community. If the rural-into-suburban small church has resented the community's "invasion" of newcomers/outsiders, however, it may become ingrown, closed to visitors, and even dysfunctional.

In each of these settings, a new singles group carries with it the possibility of bringing a breath of fresh air and "new blood" to the small church. Especially in a small church that has become dysfunctional, single adults may be just the catalyst to move the congregation to focus upon a new identity and ministry outreach. If a small church sees meaning and purpose in having a singles group (and does not see it as a "threat" to the church family), single adults can lead the way to a stronger and more balanced small church setting.[1]

Three good books that can help you better understand your task in the small church are:

• *The Small Church Is Different!* by Lyle Schaller (Nashville: Abingdon Press, 1982).

• *Activating Leadership in the Small Church* by Steve Burt (Valley Forge, PA: Judson Press, 1988).

• *Entering the World of the Small Church* by Anthony Pappas (Washington, D.C.: Alban Institute, 1988).

These resources will inspire your insight and prepare your mind-set for successful ministry development in the smaller church.

## BENEFITS OF SMALL-CHURCH SINGLES GROUPS

Singles ministries in small churches can provide a true paradigm of a caring Christian community.

**1. A smaller group allows for greater ease in getting to know one another personally.**

A large singles ministry usually struggles to find ways to create small-group settings in which people can get acquainted. Not so in the small church! You may already have the ideal size for meaningful small group dynamics. Rather than despairing that you have eight people instead of eighty, realize this can be a blessing because of the opportunity it provides to become personal. Feeling connected through relationships with other people is a cohesive characteristic of the small church setting.

**2. A small singles group provides the right backdrop for real "ministry" to**

---

## Small Churches—The Majority

Protestant churches in the United States are largely comprised of small churches, so if your church is small, you are in the majority.

According to Lyle Schaller, in *The Seven-Day-a-Week-Church,* in 1990 approximately 42% of all the people worshipping with an Evangelical Free congregation attended a church that averaged less than 200 at worship. Two thirds of those worshipping in a Church of the Nazarene congregation were in a church that averaged less than 200 worship attendance, as were 62% of those worshipping with a United Methodist congregation, 64% of those attending a United Church of Christ worship service, and 41% of those worshipping with a Missouri Synod Lutheran Church.[2]

**occur between your group members.**

The definition of ministry has nothing to do with how many people attend an event. It has everything to do with building relationships, sharing joys and concerns, offering support and prayer, and growing together spiritually, emotionally, and socially. As Jesus said, "For where two or three come together in my name, there am I with them" (Matt. 18:20). If your goal for a singles group is to minister, your goal is attainable with even a few people involved.

**3. A small singles group provides companionship and a "family" of single persons.**

The single life can feel isolated without vital connections to others. The members of small singles groups often become like a family because they learn to rely upon and trust each other, to care about each other, and to help each other in times of need.

---

*"In church (and particularly in the small church), the cohesive force is not primarily theological, geographical (neighborhood), or denominational. The primary cohesive force is shared experience. It is much like the shared experience that holds an extended family together."*
—STEVE BURT[3]

---

**4. A small church singles group often provides an intergenerational fellowship opportunity.**

Singles groups in small churches or communities regularly report that their participants vary widely in age, but that this age difference is often not an issue. Sometimes it's hard to remember who is the youngest and who is the oldest! Younger group members bring new ideas and energy. Older members provide wisdom and perspective. All ages encourage others to try new things, to think in new and healthier ways, and to appreciate others who are different than themselves.

---

*"In many small churches, the dynamics of congregational life naturally tend to bring people together in repeated face-to-face contacts across generational lines. One of the most significant implications of this generalization is that the small rural church. . .is one of the few places in American society in which the concept of intergenerational obligation is being perpetuated."* —LYLE SCHALLER[4]

---

## CHALLENGES OF SMALL-CHURCH SINGLES GROUPS

If all these benefits exist, why is it sometimes hard to create and sustain a singles group in the small church?

**1. The closely-knit "family" setting often inhibits the group from including newcomers or reaching out to new people.**

In a small or rural community, church members may be bound together by years of sharing life experiences, family histories, and long friendships. This is also true of the small church in the urban setting, whose neighborhood takes on the characteristics of a small town. If visitors try to join a singles group at a rural or urban small church, they may feel like "outsiders." The small-church group may have to work even harder than a large-church group to be friendly and intentionally open to newcomers.

**2. If the church is in a small or rural community, there are fewer single adults.**

This does not necessarily prevent the formation of a singles support group in the small church. But single adults may become discouraged because the group doesn't include more people.

**3. The small-church minister usually has difficulty just keeping the basic programs going and, subsequently, lacks time or energy to offer much support and encouragement to additional programs such as a singles ministry.**

In the small church setting, the pastor is expected to function "relationally" with pastoral care, personal contact with parishioners, and leadership of the church family. Very small churches especially are not oriented to allow the pastor a great deal of time to support, let alone develop, many new programs. Usually, the single adults of the small church must take responsibility for organizing themselves.

**4. Congregations in small church settings may resent the formation of a support group just for singles, seeing it as a possible wedge to splinter the family feeling of the small church.**

Some single adults in small churches report a complete lack of support or understanding for their attempts to have single adult activities. As in churches of any size, singles need to enlist and sustain the support of the pastor when planning a singles group. Their job is to help the pastor understand how this support group would help the church and not damage the overall family feeling of the congregation.

Small churches often believe that the proper approach to single adults is to mainstream them. But the question every small church should ask itself is: *Are we simply assuming our general church family structure is meeting the needs of single adults?*

As in the larger church, some singles will find fulfillment by integrating into the general flow of congregational life. But others benefit from the specialized support a singles group can offer.

Realize that the rewards of creating a singles group in your small church are worthwhile, but you may face challenges along the way. (But remember that a large church creating a singles ministry faces its own challenges also.)

## WHERE TO BEGIN

A small church or community wishing to begin a singles group should begin with the suggested steps in Chapters 1 and 3, answering the following questions.

### Does our church really need a singles ministry?

Answer this basic question dealt with in Chapter 1. Never skip the research process of discovering whether or not a singles ministry is actually viable, given your particular congregation and community. The basic requirements for singles ministry are the same in every setting:

- *Support from the church leadership*
- *Congregational interest and support*
- *Financial support*
- *Interested single adults.*

### Does the prevailing attitude toward singles support a singles ministry?

Establishing a positive attitude, as described in Chapter 2, is also essential. If the congregation, the pastor, or even the single adults themselves view single adults as people to pity, you will have difficulties building a healthy support group. Part of your job may be to help the church and the single adults to think positively about the single life.

### How do we get started?

After assessing your church and community situation, and if you believe the vision of the singles ministry is supported by the congregation and pastor, you are ready to recruit for the group. As mentioned in Chapter 3, you must do more than just put a note in the church bulletin, inviting single adults to attend the first gathering.

If your group is to be built on personal

▶ Please check the information in Chapter 10, "Promoting and Publicizing Your Singles Ministry," for tips on how to create your publicity in an effective and professional manner.

relationships with one another, make it a priority to contact and personally invite each single adult in your church. Do not expect the pastor to do this; take the initiative yourselves. Explain when and where the meeting will take place and why you and the church believe a singles group is important to create. If you have not previously done so, ask each person the following questions.

• *What do you think our church should be doing for single adults?*

• *What do you think about the idea of forming a singles group?*

• *What would you like to see happen in the group?*

By gaining input and ideas from each person you invite to come, you build support and ownership for the group. You will also gather data about what the participants believe should be the purpose of your group. As recommended in Chapter 3, part of the groundwork is creating a purpose statement. Do not omit this important step.

Try to extend the publicity about your new singles group into your community or area. No doubt single adults living in nearby towns, on farms in the region, and in small communities nearby (or in other parts of the metropolitan area if you're in a city) might welcome the chance to meet other people in a "safe" setting like your singles group. Put some time and research into finding out how to "get the word out." The local regional newspaper could run a feature or public service announcement about your first meeting. Radio stations will read announcements (free of charge) about events as part of their public service. Small towns and neighborhoods often offer strategic places to place flyers or posters with information. ◀

The small rural church does have a publicity benefit—the "grapevine." If the church's population is spread through a wide area, it usually has an effective, informal "word of mouth" system through which information is circulated. This will help you spread the word about your plans. Similarly, the urban small church has a "neighborhood network" through which news usually travels.

## YOUR FIRST EVENT

All singles groups, large or small, should pay close attention to guidelines for having "user-friendly" events or meetings.

### Easy to attend

Make sure your first event is located in a convenient place, in a meeting room that is clean and well-lit, and at a convenient time of day for most people. If you are meeting in a place such as the back room of a local restaurant, do not assume everyone will automatically know where the restaurant is located. Make certain that your publicity states the name of the meeting place and a general location (the north side of Main Street, for example). Local people will know where to go. But individuals from other communities or towns or parts of the city may never find your group without more specific directions in your advance publicity.

### Quality in purpose, content, and details

Make sure you host quality events. Begin and end your program on time.

---

## Adjusting Publicity Lead Time

Small churches often use a very short-term time frame for planning, since the event being planned may involve only a small number of people. However, if you would like to reach single adults beyond your immediate community, increase the "lead time" you normally allow for publicity.

Have name tags at the first event, if necessary. Think through your agenda ahead of time and plan a portion of the time for socializing, a portion for program, Bible study, or other purpose, and a portion for fellowship. Singles groups of all sizes find it very useful to read a short "purpose statement" at the beginning of each event or meeting. This sets the stage for creating the intended atmosphere for your meeting and helps new attenders understand the goals and identity of your group. By setting out your purpose at each meeting for everyone, you help build a common objective and reason for being together.

## KEYS TO SUCCESS

How can small-church singles ministries find success? The following advice was gathered from members of thriving, mature small-church singles groups. Share it with the singles in your group.

### 1. Make personal and spiritual growth your mutual goal.

If your activities have this underlying aspiration, the atmosphere when you are together will be transformed. As you give to others in the group, you will receive far more than you give. Lower your barriers and let the group members enhance each others' lives with rich friendships.

### 2. Do together what you might feel uncomfortable doing alone.

Members of a successful small group enjoy doing a variety of activities together. They support one another, by making uncomfortable "solo" projects into supported group efforts.

For example, if you're reluctant to go away on a vacation alone, rent a van with others in the group and take that long-awaited trip together. Make sure you take a camera along. The mutual memories of your adventures will be treasured.

Since your divorce, have you been self-conscious about attending the worship service on Sundays? Go to church together and sit as a group. The possibilities are endless, and the opportunities for enablement toward a fuller life are many.

### 3. Explore each others' hobbies.

One member of your group may enjoy go-cart racing. Attend one of the races as a group and learn more about the sport. Another member may be an experienced bread baker. Take a Sunday afternoon and let the chef among you demonstrate the basics of baking bread. Each group member may wish to take one month and plan the group's activity according to his or her interests.

### 4. Support each other in trying new activities.

The youngest and the oldest members of your group can benefit most from this advice. Often the encouragement of the younger ones nudges older ones into trying new ventures. And from the insight of the older, the younger discover new interests. One small singles group reports that, on one occasion, their monthly activity was a horseback riding outing. Everyone ended up riding, even the group members who were in their seventies. Without the encouragement of the others, some of the group would have never given riding a try.

A small group has the potential to become a team of people who cheer each other on to new heights of accomplishment, recreation, education, or growth.

### 5. Eat and cook together often

It's more fun to cook a big pot of chili for several people than try to make it just for one person at home alone. Potluck dinners are especially good because they give everyone a chance to contribute. Meals together are a wonderful time to have fellowship and enhance your small group's "family feeling."

### 6. Do the unexpected!

In a small church (where everything can become predictable), a surprise program, an impromptu party, or a mysterious invitation to a meeting for which the speaker remains unannounced keeps group members on their toes. Your singles group can provide the "spice" to make daily life for one another much more than just interesting.

### 7. Always present opportunities for service.

Small singles groups become ingrown and stagnant when they only exist to serve themselves. For many single adults (especially those recuperating from a life crisis like a divorce or death of a spouse), discovering ways to use their talents and time for others is part of the growth and healing process. Discuss ways members of your group can give to the church and/or the community on a regular basis.

### 8. Make prayer and prayer support the heart of your singles group.

No one in your group has to be a "spiritual giant" in order to pray for others. Having a community prayer life or a "prayer chain" is wonderfully enriching for small singles groups. Help one another learn about the art of prayer and rejoice at how God answers prayer in your lives.

### FINANCING THE SMALL CHURCH SINGLES PROGRAM

Is it possible to fund a singles group in a small church when the church budget can hardly pay the pastor? Single adults in most small churches must address this question. The answer may only be found by taking a step-by-step approach to clarifying and defining your needs and then checking a variety of available resources.◄

► See Chapter 9, Resources 26, 27 (pages 136-138) for determining financial needs.

### 1. Brainstorm with your group and make a list of realistic financial needs.

For what must you absolutely have financial resources available? Carefully look over your activity list and consider as many low- or no-cost alternatives as possible.

For example, one small-church singles group, whose own church was undergoing remodeling, rented a $20-a-month, city-owned meeting room. After struggling for some time to keep paying this rental fee, the group decided to examine other lower-cost options. Through brainstorming, the group found a small church in a neighboring community which had an adequate meeting room available at no charge. By switching locations, they eliminated the monthly rental fee and gained two single adults who were members of the other church.

### 2. Check the resources available to meet the financial needs your group has identified.

What is realistic for your group? Could each meeting include an offering which would cover monthly mailings or child care? Would speakers in the area address your group at no charge? Could anyone in the congregation donate the funds to help pay for scholarships to a singles training event? What are other ways you could cover part, if not all, of your anticipated expenses?

Some small churches tend to be more "barter" and "product services" oriented than larger congregations. In other words, members or groups within the church may be willing to exchange time and energy with each other in lieu of payment. For example, would someone from the women's church circle provide the child care for the singles event, in exchange for a few single adults' help with serving ice cream at the church social the next week? It may be possible for your group to work out certain needs (like child-care workers) through the life of the church. Check with your pastor for input and ideas.

**3. Make a projected statement of financial need to share with the pastor and the church finance committee.**

List ways your group believes it can cover certain expenses. Estimate how much money you would like the church to provide and why you feel this would be a good investment in the overall mission of the church.

You must be able to specify approximately how much money you need and why. A habit common in small singles groups is complaining that the church provides no funding—yet they have never given the church a realistic, accurate, substantiated idea of their needs. Even if the church ultimately provides little or no funding, your attempts will raise awareness about your singles group and its activities. Update your financial request statement annually and resubmit it each year. ▶

**4. Consider creating a separate, special "singles budget" which would not be part of the regular church budget.**

Research shows that special budgets receive extra attention in the small church. Often, taking a special offering on a Sunday will raise the entire amount needed. Small churches usually respond favorably to "special needs" projects, rising to the occasion if the congregation is convinced that the request is vital. Or, plan an annual fund-raising event for your singles group that can become a church tradition, like an all-church Christmas dinner or an ice cream social. Let your imaginations guide you.

**5. Continually ask God to provide your group with ideas for meeting financial needs.**

With Spirit-inspired creativity in the context of Christian fellowship, your group may develop many ways to keep the group going on the leanest budget imaginable—or even with no budget.

Remember that ministry can always occur with or without what would seem to be ideal financial support.

## TOUGH PROBLEMS FACED BY SMALL CHURCH SINGLES MINISTRIES

Small singles groups face some unique challenges. Not all of those challenges have airtight solutions. But these suggestions can help you deal with difficult situations.

**1. We have a number of single adults in our church, but most won't come to our singles group. They say they "don't need" it.**

This is a reality in a congregation of any size. Not all single adults will join a group designed specifically for single people. But in the small church, it's quite noticeable if single adults who are church members avoid participating.

Why don't they come? Consider these possibilities:

• They are meaningfully involved in other aspects of congregational life and already have found supportive friends in those activities.

• They don't like the idea of "calling attention" to their singleness by becoming involved in a singles group.

• They feel uncomfortable attending the singles group because an ex-spouse or an ex-spouse's friends or relatives are involved.

• They are waiting to see if your newly-formed singles group will succeed.

When you are planning to start a singles group, do not assume every single adult in your congregation will decide to be a member of it. And as your group is forming, do not continue to pursue single adults who clearly do not wish to become a part of your singles group. Look instead for those who would like the fellowship and support. Remember the goal of having any support group is to meet needs and provide ministry.

◀ See Chapter 9, Resource 27, page 138.

**2. The only agenda for some people in our small singles group seems to be to find a mate. This wife-and-husband hunting is a real "turn-off" for some of us.**

Single adults often put a great deal of pressure on themselves to "get married and settle down." Opportunities to meet eligible partners are limited, so naturally the singles group becomes one of the few places where single adults hope this can happen. Part of working in singles ministry is realizing that finding a life partner is a high priority for many single adults and respecting that priority.

However, that priority becomes abusive when it supersedes the stated purpose of your singles group and threatens the "safe" atmosphere of your meetings and events. A primary way to deal with this problem is to make sure your purpose statement is repeated at every event. Some groups read the purpose statement at the beginning of each event or meeting. Others use it as the basis for the opening prayer. The more you can help the group stay focused on its goals and purposes, the better you can deal with the problem of "alternate agendas" some participants may bring.

**3. We have one or two "problem personalities" in our singles group. No one likes to come to our meetings because of these individuals and there is no other singles group to send them to.**

Again, go back to your purpose statement. If your purpose is to provide a "safe place" for single adults, and a "problem personality" literally prevents that, someone in your singles group who can be kind, caring, yet firm needs to confront this person. He or she needs to understand that aggressive or inappropriate behavior is not in line with the nature of the group. That person can choose to either respect and support the group purpose or discontinue attending.

If the person with the "problem per-sonality" is not disrupting any part of the purpose of the group from happening, however, the situation is different. Any group may have an individual who is not harmful or damaging to others, but who is a "social turnoff" and does not have an effective sense of appropriate group behavior. The group may indeed be just the place for such a person to become more secure and change some of those bad habits into more appropriate ones. This is part of the ministry of Christ the church can offer—and small churches provide an "up close and personal" opportunity.

Eliminate or diminish the person's behavior by not catering to it and by actively pursuing strong leadership within the group from the "healthier" people who desire to grow and to reach out to others. The problem person is in the minority and will be increasingly so as your group grows. Not catering to the objectionable behavior will eventually force that person to decide whether to be a functioning, healthy part of the group or whether to go where he or she will receive attention for the negative behavior.

---

*"Nobody today remembers who was running the 'megachurches' of the time when St. Francis was hanging out with lepers."* —RICHARD JOHN NEUHAUS[5]

---

Again, part of "ministry" is to try to help each person find his or her place in the body of believers. The neediest will often demand the most of the group's time and attention and will become the primary focus of the group's energy if allowed. Prevent this imbalance by focusing on the people pursuing healthy lifestyles. Otherwise, your singles group will attract only the severely needy, and the stronger people will not be present to provide a nurturing, caring example.

**4. Our small church does not have enough single adults even to have a singles group. What shall the few of us do?**

If your church or community does not have enough single adults even for a small support group, consider several other options:

• *If you are in a rural area, check the resources for single adults in your county or area of the state.* Could you visit existing singles programs in a neighboring town or city? Singles from small communities often carpool to singles events in larger towns as a fellowship activity.

• *If you live in a city, find out what other singles ministries exist and consider attending some of their events together.* Take advantage of activities specifically offered for singles, whether or not they are held at your own church. Go out afterwards for coffee or a meal with the other singles from your congregation and enjoy friendship and discussion.

• *Consider creating a regional, joint singles group.* Research to find how many single adults attend churches in surrounding communities. One way to develop a singles group is to draw together singles from churches in various towns or communities or parts of the city for a monthly event.

While uniting a number of churches sounds like a great solution—and while it does offer good fellowship opportunity—it is not an easily-achieved, fool-proof plan. It is not easy to organize and sustain a ministry when several churches are sharing responsibility, when no one knows how the "end product" should look, or when the churches in the cooperative ministry are geographically far apart. The best plan of attack is to establish widespread agreement among all participating churches on exactly what will be done and who will be responsible for what. Keep it simple, so the singles activities can be enacted with a minimum of miscommunication between sponsoring churches. ▶

*4. Keep praying about your dream of ministry for and with single adults.* Seize every opportunity to minister to others, especially to single adults. Perhaps starting a singles group is in the future of your congregation.

◀ See "The Advantages of Networking with Other Churches," page 168.

## TOOLS TO HELP YOU

**Resource 33, "Small Church Singles Ministry"** *(Worksheet)* This worksheet can help you with discussion and planning as you launch a small church singles group. Don't do it alone! Make sure you have others who are helping design and establish the new venture with you.

# The Advantages of Networking with Other Churches

by Scott Bernstein and Jerry Jones

Most singles like to be with other singles where the opportunity for new relationships is enhanced. The more singles there are at a function, the greater the excitement one often experiences about being there. Since small churches have fewer singles, one of the most effective things they can do is plan events with other churches.

***1. Think interchurch.*** Many areas of singles ministry become virtual impossibilities for the small church. But when small churches join together, any dream can be realized—a retreat, a singles conference, a Friday night singles rally, or a missions trip.

***2. Think community network.*** In some areas, smaller churches have united to form a city-wide singles network with each church having representation on the council. Large events are planned by the network where all share equally in leadership and responsibility. Problems are openly shared and resolutions sought.

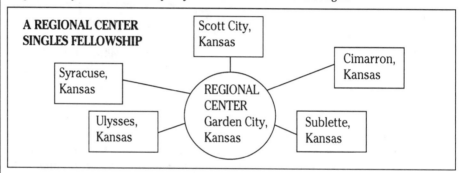

**A REGIONAL CENTER SINGLES FELLOWSHIP**

Scott City, Kansas

Cimarron, Kansas

Syracuse, Kansas

REGIONAL CENTER Garden City, Kansas

Ulysses, Kansas

Sublette, Kansas

***3. Think regional centers.*** A regional center is a natural magnet for people within a 40- to 60-mile radius. In the more sparsely populated areas of the country many people think nothing of driving fifty or more miles to do business, shop, or get medical attention in their regional center. For example (see chart above), Syracuse, Kansas has a population of approximately 2,000. It would be difficult to develop a very large Christian singles fellowship in Syracuse alone, but it is quite conceivable for people in Syracuse—as well as those from many other small communities—to drive the fifty miles to Garden City (population 35,000+) for a monthly fellowship, seminar, or gym night. If a church in Garden City sponsored a region-wide monthly get-together, the potential attendance could be 200-300 or more.

If you are a small church outside of a regional center, find a church in the center that would be willing to help sponsor such a monthly singles fellowship. Offer to help brainstorm ways to make this work. If you are a church in one of these centers, think of the potential ministry you could have by developing such a ministry for your entire region.

(Another advantage to this regional approach is that it can be less threatening for your pastor to support an out-of-town event than to support an event held at another church in your own city.)

Gather a few key people from other groups in the region. Do your planning at least six to nine months in advance. Publicize the event through local churches, bulletin boards, word of mouth, and any other options available.

There are all sorts of great things that can happen when you are willing to work together with other small groups. Together you can join forces and do some larger things and still keep that personal touch.[6]

# SMALL CHURCH SINGLES MINISTRY

**1. Have you visited with your pastor about creating a singles group at your church?**

❏ Yes  ❏ No  **If yes, date of visit** _____ *(Summarize visit below.)*

**2. Have you completed the worksheets in Chapters 1, 2, and 3?**  ❏ Yes  ❏ No

**3. Who is working on the singles ministry "dream team"?** *(See Chapter 1.)*

| Name | Phone |
|------|-------|
| _____ | _____ |
| _____ | _____ |
| _____ | _____ |
| _____ | _____ |
| _____ | _____ |
| _____ | _____ |

**4. What is the purpose statement for your singles group?** *(See Chapter 3 for guidelines on how to write a purpose statement.)*

**5. How will you publicize your new singles group?**

*(continued)*

**6. What are you planning for your first event or meeting?** *(List details.)*

Event _____ Date _____ Time_____

Place _____

**Planning Team Members' Names**                    **Phone**

_____ (Chairperson)    _____

_____                  _____

_____                  _____

_____                  _____

_____                  _____

_____                  _____

**Details**                                         **Person Responsible**

• Refreshments _____    _____

• Child care _____     _____

• Greeters _____     _____

• Agenda _____      _____

_____    _____

_____    _____

_____    _____

_____    _____

• Other _____      _____

**7. What plans have you made for financing your singles group?** *(See Chapter 9.)*

**8. How do you plan to deal with each barrier you face in creating your singles group?**
*(List each barrier and write out a plan of action for overcoming it. If necessary, use a sepa-*
*rate sheet of paper.)*

Name _____ Date _____

# Why Singles Ministries Fail and What to Do about It

REPRODUCIBLE RESOURCES AT THE END OF THIS CHAPTER

Your singles ministry has started and events are taking place. You've brought a singles program to life. But how do you keep it alive over the long run?

Many singles ministries experience an all too familiar pattern. When the ministry is new, there is a flurry of people, activity, and enthusiasm. But after a few months or years, the programs no longer seem to work and attendance dwindles. First, leaders panic. Later they become discouraged, then apathetic.

Why does this happen? How can the fire of enthusiasm be sustained? In this chapter you will find a descriptive list of seven pitfalls of single adult ministry—reasons programs flounder and sometimes fail. If you're just starting your singles ministry, take note! Or if your singles ministry is faltering, see if you can diagnose your own pitfalls.

After the pitfalls, you'll find a set of seven positive principles which should be at the heart of any singles ministry in order for it to succeed.

Each pitfall and principle is followed by a diagnostic question to help you clarify challenges in your own singles program. ◀

▶ These questions are also listed consecutively on Resource 34, "Successful Singles Ministry Checklist", page 181. Use them to evaluate your own ministry.

## SEVEN PITFALLS OF SINGLE ADULT MINISTRY

### 1. No clear direction

One church of approximately 750 members had begun a new singles ministry. The core group of singles who were planning and administering the program shared excitement, a sense of purpose, and a fairly complete idea of what they were doing and why. The initial leadership team could also articulate (both generally and specifically) where they wanted the ministry to go.

However, singles ministry leadership teams often experience the same turnover found in the group membership. At this particular church, the sense of purpose and vision held by the initial team gradually dwindled. It slipped away because each new "generation" of leaders and group members did not regularly review and update the group's purpose and direction.

As the sense of direction became muddled, people began to question why they were doing what they were doing. They started to lose the sense of having clear-cut goals, purpose, and a "targeted" ministry. Attendance began to drop and the leadership team had trouble uniting its sense of the ministry's direction.

An important key to restoring this church's singles ministry, bringing back vitality and vibrancy, was learning to keep the primary vision, purpose, and direction of the program before the leaders and attenders. This can be done in a variety of ways: through a purpose statement given to every newcomer; through inclusion of the purpose and goals in every edition of the singles newsletter; through a brief announcement at the beginning of every gathering; and through the prayers of the leadership team together. The importance of regular prayer for God's vision and leading cannot be overemphasized.

As the leadership and participants in this singles program regularly reminded themselves of their purpose statement and reason for existence, their sense of group mission and identity began to return. And they made sure that, as the leadership team experienced turnover and change, the purpose statement was reevaluated and reworked to keep current with the ministry focus.

THE QUESTION TO ASK: *"Can those involved in our singles program articulate why we have this program, what our mission statement is, and what our goals are for the ministry?"*

## 2. No opportunities for personal growth and training

Audrey had volunteered to teach the young single adult Sunday class. The singles minister gave her a Bible study booklet to use. For three months she led the young adults through the material, even though she felt inexperienced and inadequate as a teacher. At the end of three months she received in the mail a new Bible study booklet from the singles minister with a note reading, "Thanks for your great work. Here's the next book in the series. Hope you have fun!"

After three more months, Audrey finished teaching the material from the second booklet and got a phone call from the minister. "Could you please find some new material for the class? We're busy here in the church office and don't have time to get any."

Audrey's interests were beginning to pull her toward a different Sunday morning singles class, and she expressed that. "Oh, you can't quit the young singles class now!" she was told. "We don't have anyone to take your place!"

After another six weeks, Audrey quit teaching the class and left the singles ministry of that church altogether. Why? She had not received adequate opportunities for training and growth. She had burned out completely, even though she had once found the singles ministry to be a healthy and nurturing place for her.

A person can experience many types of growth—spiritual and emotional, as well as in skills for leadership skills and ministry outreach. One characteristic of a mature, healthy singles ministry is its commitment to helping leaders receive training and support for their volunteer leadership roles. This kind of ministry lets them grow in different areas of their lives.

It is easy to ask people to be responsible for programs or events, yet never give them the support, training, or resources they need to succeed and feel satisfied. Especially consider single adults who have recently endured a tragedy, disappointment, or difficulty in their lives. They need opportunities to experience success in their volunteer tasks, and they may need your help to do so. If they are asked to be involved, it is imperative that they be provided with means for growth, training, and change.

When Audrey heard that this singles ministry was offering a leadership training class on the topic of how to be a small group facilitator, she returned to the church. Since she had felt inadequate as a discussion leader, this was her chance to learn more. While taking the class, she volunteered for the hospitality committee and became a greeter for a regular singles weeknight event. Using her skills with people and her enhanced understanding of small group dynamics, Audrey joined the hospitality committee and became the trainer for new teams of greeters and follow-up callers. Through these opportunities, Audrey found satisfaction as well as spiritual, emotional, and social growth. She no longer faced burnout and a sense of inadequacy.

THE QUESTION TO ASK: *"What opportunities does our singles ministry provide for leadership development, training, and personal growth?"*

## 3. Complacency

A synonym for group or individual complacency is limited vision. This pitfall usually happens when a singles program has existed for some time and the same people have remained in leadership for an extended period. The leadership team, along with the regular attenders of the program, can form a stagnant pool of familiarity and comfortability. They become a "closed group" to newcomers who could add fresh perspectives and ideas. Has your church or singles ministry experienced this pitfall?

Nothing kills a dreamer's creativity faster than hearing leaders respond, "We've tried that before," or "We're happy as we are," or "We don't have the resources for that," or "That would never work." All of these are actually statements of complacency and limited vision.

▶ For more information about recruiting and enabling volunteer leaders, see Chapter 8.

Change requires time, energy, and work. The slide into complacency is easy. The climb out of it is difficult and frustrating. A stagnant singles group sees no new membership growth and ultimately faces dwindling attendance. The group can get the reputation of being "stuck" in certain activities and dynamics. Such a reputation is hard to change.

Complacency is especially threatening to singles ministry in the small church or town. The group may have a limited number of members without many newcomers bringing new ideas.

New people want to be involved in a singles group that is exciting and offers them a chance to be part of the action. No one wants to try to break into a group of people who have been doing the same things with the same leaders for years.

For these reasons, make sure that your leadership team serves only a certain time limit or term so that new leaders may have an opportunity to help shape and direct the activities. For some singles groups, each leader serves a year. Other groups have terms of three, six, or nine months. Let your group decide how long the leadership terms will be, then stick to the guidelines. It has been said that newcomers are "adventurers" and longtime members are "settlers." Harness the enthusiasm and insight of your "adventurers" with leadership opportunities.◀

By rotating leadership responsibilities, planning a variety of different activities each year, and keeping the purpose statement updated and prominent, ministries can avoid the pitfall of complacency.

THE QUESTIONS TO ASK: *"How are we preventing our singles ministry from sliding into complacency? What new ideas are we now seriously considering?"*

### 4. Too many changes too fast

This pitfall occurs primarily under two special circumstances. The first is when a new leadership team, full of enthusiasm and new ideas, takes over a singles program. The second is when an existing leadership team or an individual leader attends a singles ministry conference and returns overflowing with new ideas. Either way, the result is often the same. Suddenly, there are many new ideas and suggestions on the table about how to operate the singles program or how to

---

## Resistance to Change

According to church growth expert Herb Miller, 47 percent of Americans strongly resist change. "Never underestimate how strong the resistance to change will be, no matter how good your idea. On the other hand, never underestimate how much resistance to change can be eliminated by using persistent and effective reactions to those change-resisting reactions," advises Miller. His suggestions on addressing resistance to change include:
• Realizing that resistance often disappears when people become comfortable with new ideas through discussion and the passage of time.
• Helping people clarify the major differences between the "status quo" and the new idea, sharing their opinions along the way.
• Paying extra attention and listening closely to those voicing the most resistance. (Resisting change may be one way to get noticed.)
• Moving slowly but steadily, allowing the idea to take shape and the people to gain ownership.[1]

transform the existing one.

This pitfall occurs when a leader or leadership team tries to implement new ideas or changes too quickly or without sharing the vision and ownership with the rest of the group. Such changes sometimes evoke immediate resentment from others within the program. They feel their opinions have not been solicited or respected in the decision-making process.

Part of effective change is seeking input from those involved and spreading ownership and vision for the changes among the group. Radical and sudden changes without mutual consent and group support almost guarantee a downward spiral.

New ideas and changes are essential, but they must be accompanied by adequate time, preparation, and communication.

One way to bring everyone "on board" with new ideas is to have quarterly brainstorming sessions for anyone involved in the singles ministry. At these sessions, explain and discuss new ideas or changes.

If new directions for the program are approved, succinctly explain them in the singles newsletter or during the announcement time at the next singles event. Those who don't like the changes but failed to attend the planning sessions forfeited their chance for preliminary input.

THE QUESTIONS TO ASK: *"What route of approval does a suggested change in our singles program go through before it is put into effect? How are we encouraging and allowing input from group members?"*

## 5. Low quality or poor performance

Over the last forty to fifty years, our society has changed dramatically—and so has the church. At one time in America, the church was the spiritual, social, and recreational center of the community. However, with the onset of more free-time options, the church has become only one of the endless alternatives competing for people's attention. Health clubs, learning institutions, recreational groups, social clubs, and even television offer other outlets for involvement, education, and entertainment. No longer can the church claim priority by virtue of its traditional favored status.

If the church wants to compete with high-quality secular events, it must respond to people's interests and needs with care, professionalism, and precision. Churches cannot get by without preparation or organization. If the church wants to reach into the community, its programs and materials must have quality. Consider an example of this pitfall, illustrated by the experience of a professional speaker who was scheduled for a singles meeting. The meeting was to begin at 7:00 P.M. The speaker was the first person to arrive. At 7:05 P.M. the first member of the singles program showed up. By 7:15 P.M. the rest of the group arrived. The room had not been set up ahead of time—no chairs and registration table, no signs were posted to direct newcomers, no greeters were at the doors. No one came early to meet the speaker and find out whether he needed an easel, overhead projector, or other supplies. These failures all point to carelessness and poor-quality follow-through.

Doing basic groundwork is imperative to hosting a quality event. If participants attend a haphazardly-planned program, they'll feel their valuable time has been wasted. Visitors will usually not return to a singles ministry if the event they attend doesn't make a quality, caring, well-planned impression. ▶

NOTE: Even if only one key person's involvement in the program is unprofessional or of poor quality, it can affect the whole mood of the event. Help the leadership team members each contribute to an

◀ If your singles ministry struggles with this pitfall, see Chapter 5, "Creating Quality Events."

event according to their unique abilities and gifts. Certain individuals may do a great job giving announcements and introducing the speaker, while others perform most effectively as greeters, organizing the table and chair set-up arrangement, preparing refreshments, or providing child care.

A myth among some Christian circles seems to say that even when a volunteer's performance in a task is not suited to his or her abilities, the "Christian" attitude is to put up with it. However, the most loving response is actually to help the person find where and how to most effectively share personal talents or spiritual gifts in the context of the ministry program.

THE QUESTIONS TO ASK: *"Is poor quality a common or rare occurrence in our singles ministry? What are we doing to match tasks and responsibilities with those who are most gifted in each area?"*

## 6. Poor delegation

Leaders in church ministry, whether lay or professional, often feel a sense of urgency to arrange many details within a limited time frame. A pitfall can result if one of two possible scenarios takes place.

• *The leader chooses to "take care" of things and completely skips involving others with preparations, thus creating no group ownership, resulting in poor group attendance or low group interest.*

• *The leader recruits anyone to help, regardless of abilities or talents.* The task is then carried out in a less than professional manner by people who don't really want to do what they are doing. ◀

Real ministry takes place by helping people discover their abilities and talents and inviting them to share those gifts. Instead of just trying to recruit anyone who will say yes, leadership should clarify the gifts or skills needed for a par-

▶ Is poor delegation a pitfall of your singles ministry leadership? Review how leadership style can facilitate better group involvement (see Chapter 8).

ticular task and invite individuals to serve accordingly. Delegating the leadership and ownership appropriately is the only way to keep the group healthy and prevent overcontrol by one or a few leaders.

*The leaders of your singles ministry will determine the quality of your group—in terms of programs, image, and outreach.* ("What you radiate is what you attract.") Their attitude toward involving others and helping create exciting activities for single adults is a barometer which reveals your program's success (or failure).

THE QUESTION TO ASK: *"How effectively does our singles ministry leadership delegate authority?"*

## 7. Poor communication

It has been cryptically stated that the greatest misconception about communication is that it has taken place! Many times leaders think they have effectively communicated vision, direction, and purpose. But days or weeks later, they discover the people with whom they had spoken received a completely different perception of the situation.

Because communication is so important, leaders must constantly reiterate the ministry's goals, purpose, and direction to those involved in the program. In addition, regularly staying in touch with the key committee chairpersons is vital. This can be done through meetings, phone calls, notes, or an occasional cup of coffee together. The more frequently and clearly they receive communication, the more they will understand the heartbeat of the ministry.

Poor communication is also common between the singles ministry and the church as a whole. Jim Smoke, founder of The Center for Divorce Recovery in Phoenix, Arizona, cites "unfounded congregational fears" as one reason singles ministries can fail. "The failure of the congregation to understand the ministry and its goals will raise such a wall of doubt and questioning that the ministry will self-destruct. People fear what they don't understand. A ministry must be interpreted and explained to the congregation in order to gain its vital support and encouragement."[2]

THE QUESTIONS TO ASK: *"How would we rate the effectiveness of communication between leadership and participants in our singles program? Between the singles ministry and the whole church?"*

## SEVEN POSITIVE PRINCIPLES OF SINGLE ADULT MINISTRY

Successful singles programs not only work to avoid the deadly pitfalls listed above, but also strive to implement life-giving, positive principles about ministry. Here are some common characteristics or principles that vibrant, successful singles ministry programs all share.

### 1. Clear convictions

Successful singles ministries know what they believe and minister from their convictions.

Some say churches today are having an identity crises because they concentrate on the wrong things. Churches spend large quantities of time and money deciding what hymnal to use, what brand of computer to buy for the office secretaries, and which Sunday class gets to use which classroom on Sunday mornings. When energies are diverted to such lesser concerns, churches gradually lose their identity and sense of greater purpose. Gradually, they become congregations of people in power struggles over small issues. Accordingly, they become completely out of touch with the great visions which have kept the church alive and clearly connected to the Great Commission of Jesus Christ.

*Approximately 350,000 congregations exist in our country. More than 60,000 of these report that they have not gained one convert during a year's time. What is happening to our churches and the cutting edge of the Gospel?*
—REPORTED IN BIBLIOTHECA SACRA[3]

The churches across the country—around the world—that are growing and seeing lives changed are the churches that know what they believe, keep that purpose in mind, and offer ministries based on those convictions. This keeps them from becoming empty social scenes, humanitarian service clubs, or political forums. Healthy ministry includes fellowship, helping others, and the mandate to impact society and government, but ministries must first incorporate the convictions of the Christian faith into the lives of their members.

Our singles ministries must also be ministries based upon conviction. Unless lives are transformed by the Gospel of Jesus Christ, authentic ministry in God's name is not taking place.

THE QUESTION TO ASK: *"Is our singles ministry based upon the transforming power of the Gospel of Christ?"*

### 2. Opportunities for personal growth and training

Successful singles ministries breed success by allowing for failure.

Many times in the increasingly competitive world of church ministry, the pressure to perform is so great that people don't volunteer for fear of failure. They will not feel safe committing their time and energy to help until they see the singles ministry as a safe place for growth, exploration, and affirmation.

An experienced singles minister in

charge of a large program faced a situation that demonstrated this principle. The minister asked a participant to accept a specific leadership role. But after a few months, the volunteer was failing badly in the position and was feeling discouraged. Wisely, the singles minister gave him a graceful way to bow out of the leadership responsibility with dignity.

Six months later, the minister asked the same individual to be in leadership again—in a different area of the program. The participant was shocked. "I failed so miserably before. Why are you asking me to try again?" he asked.

"I share the responsibility for your failure," the minister answered. "I didn't help set you up to succeed the first time by helping you identify your personal gifts and talents and asking you to serve accordingly. I think serving in this new part of the program may just be suited to all you have to contribute."

The man accepted the new position and succeeded wonderfully. He was given the opportunity to succeed by being allowed the possibility of failure.

THE QUESTION TO ASK: **"Is our singles ministry set up to allow failure, in order to help people learn to succeed?"**

### 3. Strong support system

Successful in singles ministries gain and sustain the support of the senior pastor and congregation.

As mentioned in Chapter 1, launching and maintaining a growing singles ministry is very difficult without the senior pastor's support and advocacy. You should also seek and cultivate the support of key lay leadership in various committees throughout the church. Without this support system, your ministry will face a perpetual uphill battle.

If gaining such support seems unlikely, evaluate why the church does not want to

offer that support. The lack of support will be sensed by the single adults who visit your church. There is no substitute for good, continual communication with the senior pastor and congregation about the single adult ministry.

THE QUESTION TO ASK: **"Does our singles program have the support of the senior pastor and key church leadership?"**

### 4. Group members tapped as resources

Successful singles ministries must recruit from within their own ranks to equip and train workers for leadership. This is important because it gives the ministry ownership for itself, it keeps the people who are involved communicating with each other, and it keeps everyone accountable. Rather than having the attitude of, "When will someone come and help teach, lead, organize, or minister to us singles?" the attitude becomes, "How can I contribute to our singles ministry?" An internally-fed singles ministry gives all involved a sense of supporting, encouraging, and building one another.

For example, one key in drawing upon the resources of the single adults might be to invite them to complete "interest indicators" on which they list occupation, hobbies, and interests. Enlisting volunteers for responsibilities compatible with their interests is easier to manage. And those volunteers are more likely to find growth and fulfillment through the time and energy they invest in the ministry.

THE QUESTION TO ASK: **"How much do we draw our resources from the single adults with whom we minister?"**

### 5. Balanced program

Successful singles ministries are action-oriented but carefully balance their activities to regularly offer opportunity for spiritual, intellectual, emotional, and social growth.

If you are starting a brand-new singles group, it is impossible to spring full-blown into existence; every program must begin on a well-targeted basis. However, as the program develops over time, a balanced look to the slate of weekly and monthly plans should take shape.

Chris Eaton, Executive Director of Single Purpose Ministries in St. Petersburg, Florida, has written on the subject of building a well-balanced singles ministry in *Singles Ministry Handbook*.[4]

According to his experience as a singles leader, imbalance in a singles program usually tends toward these two extremes:

• *Singles group focused primarily on spiritual issues and study—with little or no social activities.*

• *Singles group focused primarily on social interaction—with no sense of meaningful community based on a solid foundation.*

In a singles program, balance usually begins with the leadership team's sensitivity and flexibility. The leadership should plan events and activities which holistically address singles' needs—spiritually, emotionally, intellectually, and socially.

THE QUESTION TO ASK: *"Does our singles ministry have a 'balanced' calendar of events each month?"*

## 6. In touch

Successful singles ministries stay in touch with the people in their ministry.

The importance of good communication cannot be overemphasized for successful ministry. Staying in touch with the leaders (and participants) in the program goes beyond basic communication about scheduled events and meetings. For effective ministry, you must be a friend and a colleague in the common cause of the ministry.

One single adult volunteer began a singles group in her church. But after five months she quit attending the events because she had entered a dating relationship and no longer felt "single." However, she refused to relinquish her leadership role. For the next year she "directed" the program, planned the activities, organized the details of events, yet never showed up to meet the people, to hear their ideas, or to build community. She was later shocked to hear that "another" singles group was forming in her church. Her refusal to relate to and with the participants effectively stifled any hope for the original group to thrive.

Rich Hurst, former singles minister at the Crystal Cathedral in Garden Grove, California, says his best communication with people in leadership comes from regularly asking each, "How are you doing and what are your dreams?" That simple question gives the invitation for true communication—not just Rich informing the leader about programs and responsibilities, but the leader sharing joys and concerns with him. It helps him establish relationships with the volunteer leaders and participants in the singles ministry.

In her powerful book *Turning Committees into Communities*, Roberta Hestenes contends that committees and task forces work best when they transcend the "all business" agenda and become a group of people who care and share together.[5]

---

*"Ideally, the role of the church is not to push people into programs, but to assist people in realizing who they are and how to share their lives with others."*
—GEORGE BARNA[6]

---

One job of the singles ministry worker is sensing the "emotional barometer" in meetings. Do participants look tense or tired? Are one or two radiating with "I have good news!" and need an opportunity to tell about their week? Being sensitive to sharing the load and walking the extra mile with your ministry participants helps develop a strong sense of communication.

THE QUESTIONS TO ASK: *"How well does the leadership of our singles ministry stay in touch and form community together? How well are we communicating with (and listening to) the singles in our group?"*

### 7. Great Commission—the goal

Successful singles ministries keep Jesus' call in the Great Commission first and foremost.

*"All authority in heaven and on earth has been given to me. Therefore go and make disciples of all nations, baptizing them in the name of the Father and of the Son and of the Holy Spirit, and teaching them to obey everything I have commanded you. And surely I am with you always, to the very end of the age."*
—JESUS (MATT. 28:18-20)

Always remember that the singles ministry should tie in with the overall mission of the church rather than assuming a completely separate mission of its own. While single adult ministry is a specialized area, it still must contain solid biblical teaching, be founded on the importance and power of prayer, and follow the call of Christ to make disciples.

The challenge of those in Christian ministry to single adults is to help open doors for God's Spirit to transform lives.

*"Individual renewal is indissolubly connected to the renewal of the whole church. We cannot attain the fullness of the Spirit without being turned inside out so that our central focus is no longer our own growth, but the glory of God and the growth of Christ's kingdom."*
—RICHARD LOVELACE[7]

THE QUESTION TO ASK: *"How effectively does our singles ministry follow the Great Commission?"*

## TOOLS TO HELP YOU

How does your singles ministry rate? What are the strengths and weaknesses in your existing program? How would you like to plan for the future in order to incorporate positive ministry principles into your work?

• **Resource 34, "Successful Singles Ministry Checklist"** *(Evaluation Guide)* Use this evaluation worksheet as a discussion guide for your leadership team. Discuss these questions every three to six months (or whenever the membership of the leadership/planning team changes) in order to keep yourselves sensitive to what you're doing and why.

# SUCCESSFUL SINGLES MINISTRY CHECKLIST
### (Evaluation Guide for Leadership Teams)

1. In what ways does your ministry regularly state its purpose? *(Can the people in your ministry articulate its direction?)*

2. What opportunities does the ministry provide for leadership development and personal growth?

3. Is your singles program characterized by complacency? ❑ Yes ❑ No  How can you prevent complacency among the leadership and participants in your group?

4. What procedure does a suggested change in the program undergo before it is put into effect?  How many people have the opportunity to help "own" the decision for change or new programming before it happens?

5. Is poor quality and poor performance common or rare in your program?

6. How effectively does your ministry leadership delegate responsibility?

7. Would you rate the communication effectiveness among the leadership and the people in your program as excellent, good, fair, or poor? Why? How would you rate communication effectiveness between the singles ministry and the church as a whole?

*(continued)*

8. Is your singles ministry based upon the transforming power of the Gospel of Christ? How is this message reflected at the heart of all aspects of your singles ministry?

9. Is your singles ministry set up to allow failure, in order to help people learn to succeed? *(Explain.)*

10. Does your senior pastor support the singles ministry? What can you do to gain this support or keep it strong?

11. Are you effectively recruiting from within your own ranks to equip and train workers for volunteer leadership? What could be done to strengthen this area?

12. Do you have a "balanced" calendar of events each month? In what ways would you like to become more balanced?

13. How well does the ministry leadership stay in touch and form community with each other?

14. How effectively does your singles ministry follow the Great Commission of Christ? *(Matthew 28:18-20)*

# Appendix:
# Tools for the Leader

So you're just starting a singles ministry? Here are a few tools to help you feel more competent for the job.

# HOW TO HOLD EFFECTIVE MEETINGS

Church leadership and planning meetings have acquired a bad reputation over the years—usually for good reason. Nothing subdues enthusiasm more than long, boring meetings. Three major complaints about church meetings are that they last too long, they are uninteresting, and they are mostly a waste of time with very little accomplished.

The obvious solution is to create meetings that are short, exciting, and a good investment of time. How do we make our meetings more effective and enjoyable?

## SIX STEPS FOR SUCCESSFUL MEETINGS

1. **Make copies of "general announcements" and "new agenda items" available to all participants at least one day before the meeting.**
   This minimizes time needed during your actual meeting, since the sharing of announcements does not have to be done verbally. Alerting the attenders of new agenda items in advance lets them think through the topics and increases the likelihood that they will have ideas and input ready.

2. **Open the meeting with acknowledgments of accomplishments.**
   People volunteer because they want to be part of something significant. They want to know their involvement makes a difference. The leader must let them know they are having an effect. Begin the meeting by showing appreciation to individuals as well as to the whole group for the quality work they have done. (**NOTE:** To evaluate whether volunteer work has been successful, ask yourself the following questions.)
   - Has the work been done within the guidelines of the church's ministry?
   - Has the work been done on time?
   - Has the work been done in such a way that it has not interfered with other parts of the ministry and has enhanced the whole project or program?

3. **Ask two important questions of the group members.**
   - What has happened since our last meeting that you are the most excited about in your area of the singles ministry?
   - What has happened since our last meeting that you are least excited about in your area of the singles ministry?
   These two questions set the direction for discussing what you are doing right as a group—and what you are doing wrong. Remember, this is not a time to focus on individual performance, but on the team. Do not let this turn into a complaint session. Rather, use the responses as a springboard into the next phase of the meeting.

4. **Follow up on the last meeting.**
   Take a look at the action plan from your last meeting. Every effective meeting should have an action plan. The action plan contains the following information:
   - What needs to be done?
   - Who will take responsibility?
   - What resources do we need to accomplish our goal?

*(continued)*

An action plan identifies who is responsible for the tasks, activities, or program ahead. It also provides a sense of accountability and a link from one meeting to the next.

If your last meeting did not have an action plan, create one during every meeting in the future. If you did previously have an action plan, review it as a group and use it to form a new action plan.

Does discussion of the old action plan tend to turn into a "moan and groan" session? Prevent this by discussing problems only long enough to identify the difficulty and its cause. Making such a diagnosis helps shift the discussion to the next step.

## 5. Make a new action plan.

What projects are continuing? Which ones are beginning? Answer the three action plan questions as a group: What needs to be done? Who will take responsibility? What resources do we need to accomplish our goal?

## 6. Provide for professional development.

One reason people don't volunteer is that they don't know how to do what they have been asked to do. In each meeting, allow a short time of personal and professional ministry development. Watch a video portion, listen to part of an audio tape, have a guest speaker, or hand out an article. Then briefly discuss the content and implications for ministry. Do something that enhances each person's ability to minister with single adults.

It helps keep enthusiasm going to let different members of the meeting plan the professional development time. They feel more motivated to read and learn themselves when they are helping the whole leadership group grow in ministry competence.

---

## Characteristics of Poor Meetings

**Why are so many meetings boring, unproductive—and almost always too long? Here are a few of the reasons.**

- "No specific, clear-cut 'objective' for the meeting, its leaders, or its participants.

- No meeting agenda.

- Too many or the wrong choice of participants.

- No consideration for allies or antagonists.

- Failure to prepare properly.

- Inability to present ideas concisely.

- Lack of sound leadership and control.

- Improper use of visual aids.

- Too many digressions and interruptions.

- Time wasted on 'why' rather than 'how.'

- Mixed final decisions."

—Milo O. Frank, *How to Run a Successful Meeting in Half the Time*, (New York: Simon and Schuster, 1989), page 18.

---

*(continued)*

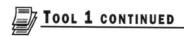 

## ADDITIONAL "WORDS TO THE WISE" REGARDING MEETINGS

1. **Hold committee or team meetings at least once a month.**
Regularly scheduled meetings will help to build continuity and community among the members.

2. **Set a time limit for your meetings.**
Committee members become burned out when meetings drag on for hours. In most cases, everything that needs to be accomplished can occur within one to one and a half hours. If the members know time is limited, they tend to work together more effectively. Let the people attending the meeting know you will start and end on time, and stick to the time limit that has been set.

3. **Designate a "recorder" to take notes on the action plan.**
Keep reasonable records of your meetings to ensure that you do not repeat "old ground" at every meeting and that you keep track of who has responsibility for which tasks.

4. **Intentionally avoid traditional terms like "old business" and "new business."**
By focusing upon the action plan concept, your meeting will emphasize the action elements of accomplishing tasks and look more easily ahead to what needs to be done—rather than endlessly discussing "old business" details. This will give a more dynamic feel to your meetings.

5. **Keep the lines of communication open and help each committee member feel connected with the whole.**
Communicate with the team or committee members through phone calls, cards, coffee together, or other means.

---

### How Did It Go?

**How do you know if your meeting has been successful?** Evaluating your meeting will help make the next one even more effective. Ask yourselves these questions afterward:

**1. What happened?** Did we get the results we wanted? What did we accomplish? What problems were solved? What decisions did the group make? Did we see progress?

**2. How did the meeting go?** How were problems solved? How were decisions made? How well did the group work together? How did people feel about the meeting?

—from *How to Make Meetings Work* by Michael Doyle and David Straus (New York: Jove Books, 1976), page 7.

---

# PRINCIPLES OF HELPING A LEADERSHIP TEAM WORK TOGETHER

**Whether you build an existing team or start a new team, these eight principles can help team members work together.**

### PRINCIPLE 1
Always be willing to do more than your share.

### PRINCIPLE 2
Refrain from saying uncomplimentary things about another team member behind his or her back.

### PRINCIPLE 3
Accept reality. All members do not have the same duties. Not everyone on a team can do the same things.

### PRINCIPLE 4
Participate in team activities even when it is inconvenient to do so. When you agree to be a team member, you agree to be connected and accountable to teammates. This is not always convenient. Make every effort to be a team player.

### PRINCIPLE 5
Confront your conflicts. Every team will experience conflicts. It is a normal and healthy part of team development. But when those conflicts go unaddressed they become destructive. When we commit to resolve conflicts it strengthens team relationships.

### PRINCIPLE 6
Don't be late or absent for trivial reasons.

### PRINCIPLE 7
Be involved, concerned, and active in your own personal growth. Team development and personal growth cannot be separated.

### PRINCIPLE 8
Contribute to the personal growth of other team members whenever it is appropriate. You contribute to the personal growth of others through sharing resources and information.

—from *Singles Ministry Resource Notebook '92-'93*, page 16, as adapted from the book, *Giving the Ministry Away*, by Terry Hershey, Karen Butler, and Rich Hurst (Elgin, IL: David C. Cook Publishing Co., 1992).

# WHAT TO SAY TO A PROSPECTIVE VOLUNTEER

### (SUMMARY FROM CHAPTER 8)

Many leaders shy away from inviting people to volunteer because they aren't sure what to say and how to say it. Offering an invitation is not difficult, but it does call for some thought. And you must believe that what you're asking the volunteer to do is a worthwhile task.

| **DO SAY** | **DO NOT SAY** |
|---|---|
| These simple, clear phrases *do* belong in what you say to a prospective volunteer. | The following phrases *do not* belong in your invitation to a prospective volunteer. |

**DO SAY**

- "We are looking for someone with real gifts in this area for this responsibility."
- "Do you have interests in this area?"
- "How can we help you contribute some of your talents to the singles ministry programs?"
- "Would you like to. . .?" (instead of, "Could you. . ." or "Would you be willing. . .?")
- "I've noticed you seem to be gifted in this area. . . ."

**DO NOT SAY**

- "I know you're busy, but. . ."
- "Would you mind doing a little thing for our program?"
- "We're desperate for new people to help us. We really need you to say yes."
- "Could you at all possibly do this?"
- "We can't find anybody else to do it. . . ."

**Never apologize for inviting a volunteer to help.** Don't say, "I can guess that you are probably too busy to help us, but I'd like to ask anyway. . . ." By apologizing, you communicate that the volunteer probably has something else more important to do, or that what you're asking them to do is not worthwhile. Make your invitation to volunteer positive, simple, and straightforward.

**Do not minimize or downplay the actual responsibilities of the task you are inviting the volunteer to do.** People want to feel their volunteer work is important. Represent the parameters of the task realistically and fairly.

Here are the three things a volunteer wants to know.

1. **Will this job be meaningful?** Does it fulfill God's plan? Will I feel a sense of significance?
2. **Will I have authority and structure?** What is the chain of command? Will I have the freedom to get things done?
3. **What about training?** How will I effectively learn what I've been asked to do?

**Always remember the importance of caring for the individuals you invite to volunteer, whether they say yes or no.** God's love is extended through your willingness to listen, to support, and to understand those with whom you minister. Your willingness to form relationships with volunteers and to appreciate them and their work may empower them for future service.

# FACTS ABOUT LEADERS OF SINGLE ADULT MINISTRIES

Who are the leaders in single adult ministries today? What are their challenges? What single adult issues and topics do they believe most need to be addressed today?

To answer those questions, *Single Adult Ministries Journal* surveyed hundreds of single adult leaders across the country. Here's what they found, as reported in *Singles Ministry Resources Notebook '92-'93,* page 10.

## What Issues and Topics Do Your Singles Adults Most Need Addressed?

The top ten answers from singles ministry leaders were:

1. Spiritual growth/relationship with God.
2. Skills for developing close personal relationships.
3. How to develop and nurture a sense of community/belonging.
4. Developing a personal ministry (giving of self to others).
5. Living with inadequate finances.
6. Tie: Adult dating; Lack of self-esteem.
7. Tie: Growing through divorce; How to be a more effective single parent.
8. Tie: Life goals/planning; Discouragement and depression about not being married; Sex/physical intimacy.
9. Materialistic influences.
10. Relationship with one's ex-spouse.

## What Is the Most Frustrating Aspect of Being a Leader in Singles Ministry?

The top ten answers from singles ministry leaders were:

1. Lack of commitment among the singles.
2. The constant need and challenge to recruit and develop leadership in the ministry.
3. High turnover rate of the single adults.
4. Too little time for personal renewal.
5. Lack of interest in spiritual growth among the singles.
6. Finding good curriculum and study discussion materials.
7. Lack of a personal support system.
8. So many depression problems/needs among the singles.
9. Tie: Heavy counseling load; An inadequate singles ministry budget.
10. Tie: The extent of inappropriate sexual activity of some of the singles; Inadequate personal income and benefits.

# SINGLES MINISTRY BIBLIOGRAPHY

## MUST-READ BOOKS

Although many excellent resources are listed in this bibliography, three resources (besides *Starting a Single Adult Ministry*) are "must-reads" for anyone who wants to start a singles ministry. All are published by David C. Cook Publishing Co., Elgin, Illinois.
- *Growing Your Single Adult Ministry*, Jerry Jones (ed.), 1991.
- *The Idea Catalog for Single Adult Ministry*, Jerry Jones (ed.), 1991.
- *Developing a Divorce Recovery Ministry,* by Bill Flanagan, 1992.

## SINGLES MINISTRY LEADERSHIP RESOURCES

Collier-Stone, Kay. *Single in the Church.* Washington, D.C.: Alban Institute, 1992.

Fagerstrom, Douglas. *Singles Ministry Handbook.* Wheaton, IL: Victor Books, 1989.

_____. *Single Adult Ministry: The Next Step.* Wheaton, IL: Victor Books, 1993.

Hershey, Terry. *Young Adult Ministry.* Loveland, CO: Group Books, 1986.

_____, Karen Butler, and Rich Hurst. *Giving the Ministry Away.* Elgin, IL: David C. Cook Publishing Co., 1992.

Jones, Jerry, ed. *Growing Your Single Adult Ministry.* Elgin, IL: David C. Cook Publishing Co., 1991.

_____. *The Idea Catalog for Single Adult Ministry.* Elgin, IL: David C. Cook Publishing Co., 1991.

Patterson, Sheron. *Ministry with Black Single Adults.* Nashville, TN: Discipleship Resources, 1990.

Reed, Bobbie. *Single on Sunday: A Manual for Successful Single Adult Ministry.* St. Louis, MO: Concordia Publishing House, 1979.

Westfall, John, and Bobbie Reed. *Let Go: A Fresh Look at Effective Leadership in Ministry.* San Diego, CA: Single Adult Ministry Associates, 1990.

## DIVORCE

Bustanoby, Andre. *But I Didn't Want a Divorce.* Grand Rapids, MI: Zondervan, 1978.

Flanagan, Bill. *Developing a Divorce Recovery Ministry.* Elgin, IL: David C. Cook Publishing Co., 1992.

Hershey, Terry. *Beginning Again: Life after a Relationship Ends.* Nashville, TN: Thomas Nelson, 1986.

Morphis, Doug. *Divorce Recovery Workshop.* Nashville, TN: Discipleship Resources, 1986. (Both student and leader's guide available.)

Smoke, Jim. *Growing Through Divorce.* Eugene, OR: Harvest House, 1986.

_____. *Suddenly Single.* Old Tappan, NJ: Revell, 1982.

Vigveno, H.S., and Anne Claire. *No One Gets Divorced Alone: How Divorce Affects Moms, Dads, Kids, and Grandparents.* Venture, CA: Regal Books, 1987.

## CHILDREN OF DIVORCE

Cynaumon, Greg. *Helping Single Parents with Troubled Kids: A Ministry Resource for Pastors and Youth Workers.* Elgin, IL: David C. Cook Publishing Co., 1992.

Dycus, Jim and Barbara. *Children of Divorce.* Elgin, IL: David C. Cook Publishing Co., 1987.

Hart, Archibald. *Children and Divorce.* Nashville, TN: Word, 1989.

Johnson, Laurene, and Georglyn Rosenfeld. *Divorced Kids: What You Need to Know to Help Kids Survive a Divorce.* Nashville, TN: Thomas Nelson, 1990.

Murray, Steve, and Randy Smith. *Divorce Recovery for Teenagers.* Grand Rapids, MI: Zondervan, 1990.

Newman, George. *101 Ways to Be a Long-Distance Superdad.* Saratoga, CA: R & E Publishing, 1981.

Schiller, Barbara. *Just Me & the Kids: Building Healthy Single-Parent Families.* Elgin, IL: David C. Cook Publishing Co., 1994.

Wallerstein, Judith. *Second Chances: Men, Women, and Children a Decade after Divorce.* New York, NY: Ticknor and Fields, 1989.

## SINGLE PARENTING ISSUES
Barnes, Robert. *Single Parenting: A Wilderness Journey.* Carol Stream, IL: Tyndale House, 1988.

Reed, Bobbie. *The Single Parent Journey: Thirteen-Session Study of Needs/Issues/Solutions.* Anderson, IN: Warner Press, 1992.

Reed, Bobbie. *Single Mothers Raising Sons.* Nashville, TN: Thomas Nelson, 1988.

Richmond, Gary. *Successful Single Parenting.* Eugene, OR: Harvest House, 1990.

Schiller, Barbara. *Just Me & the Kids: Building Healthy Single-Parent Families.* Elgin, IL: David C. Cook Publishing Co., 1994.

## GRIEF
Luehering, Carol. *Helping a Child Grieve and Grow.* St. Meinrad, IN: Abbey Press, 1990.

Manning, Doug. *Don't Take My Grief Away.* New York, NY: Harper and Row, 1984.

Sanford, Doris. *The Comforter: A Journey through Grief.* Sisters, OR: Multnomah, 1989.

Westberg, Granger. *Good Grief.* Minneaplolis, MN: Augsburg Fortress Publishers, 1979.

## RELATIONSHIP ISSUES
Hershey, Terry. *Clear-Headed Choices in a Sexually Confused World.* Loveland, CO: Group Books, 1988.

_____. *Intimacy: The Longing of Every Human Heart.* Eugene, OR: Harvest House, 1984.

Jones, Jerry. *201 Great Questions: Conversation Starters for Times with Friends.* Colorado Springs, CO: NavPress, 1988.

Jones, Thomas. *Sex and Love When You're Single Again.* Nashville, TN: Thomas Nelson, 1990.

McDowell, Josh. *The Secret of Loving: How a Lasting Intimate Relationship Can Be Yours.* Nashville, TN: Here's Life Publishers, 1985.

Rink, Margaret. *Can Christians Love Too Much? Breaking the Cycle of Codependency.* Grand Rapids, MI: Zondervan, 1989.

## SINGLENESS

Greenwaldt, Karen. *For Everything There Is a Season: A Book of Meditations for Single Adults.* Nashville, TN: Discipleship Resources, 1988.

Reed, Bobbie. *Learn to Risk: Finding Joy As a Single Adult.* Grand Rapids, MI: Zondervan, 1990.

Smith, Harold Ivan. *Fortysomething and Single.* Wheaton, IL: Victor Books, 1991.

## SMALL GROUP/STUDY GROUP CURRICULUM

***Christian LifeStyle Series.*** Elgin, IL: David C. Cook Publishing Co.
Small group resource materials, complete with reproducible resource sheets, include the following titles:
- *Attacking Your Me-Attitudes* (1991)
- *Facing Your Fears about Sharing Your Faith* (1991)
- *Giving the Body a Lift by Using Your Spiritual Gift* (1993)
- *Jump-Starting Your Devotional Life* (1991)
- *Living the Toughest Teachings of Jesus* (1991)
- *Sharpening Your Everyday Ethics* (1991)
- *Walking with God When You Have Feet of Clay* (1991)

***LifeTopics Studies.*** Elgin, IL: David C. Cook Publishing Co.
Small group resource material based upon popular Christian books, complete with coordinating Scripture study and reproducible resource sheets. Titles include:
- *Stress Fractures (1991)*
- *Balancing Life's Demands (1991)*
- *Total Life Management (1991)*
- *Bruised but Not Broken (1991)*
- *Parenting Alone (1993)*

***Lifestyle Small Group Series.*** Colorado Springs, CO: NavPress (Serendipity House), 1989. Titles of separate small group discussion guides (6-8 week sessions each) include:
- *Career*
- *Money*
- *Success*
- *Family*
- *Singles*
- *Transitions*
- *Lifestyles*
- *Stress*
- *Wholeness*

Swindoll, Lucy. *Celebrating Life: Catching the Thieves That Steal Your Joy.* Colorado Springs, CO: NavPress, 1989.

## VIDEO RESOURCES

Morgan, Andy. *Divorce Recovery*. Grand Rapids, MI: Say What Communications, 1991.

Smalley, Gary. *Hidden Keys to Loving Relationships*. Paoli, PA: Relationships Today, Inc., 1991.

Smith, Harold Ivan. *One Is a Whole Number*. Muskegon, MI: Gospel Films, 1985.

Smoke, Jim. *Forgiveness*. Grand Rapids, MI: Say What Communications, 1993.

*DivorceCare*. Raleigh, NC: DivorceCare, 1994.

## SMALL CHURCH MINISTRY

Burt, Steve. *Activating Leadership in the Small Church*. Valley Forge, PA: Judson Press, 1988.

Pappas, Anthony. *Entering the World of the Small Church*. Washington, D.C.: Alban Institute, 1988.

Schaller, Lyle. *The Small Church Is Different!* Nashville, TN: Abingdon Press, 1982.

# END NOTES

## CHAPTER 1

[1] Terry Hershey, as stated at a Singles Ministry Resources Leadership Training Group Seminar in Lincoln, Nebraska, March 15, 1991.

[2] Robert Pierson, "Effective Singles Ministry Principles," *Net Results* (Lubbock, TX: National Evangelistic Association of the Christian Church [Disciples of Christ]), June 1992, 1.

[3] George Barna, *Single Adults in America* (Glendale, CA: Barna Research Group, 1987), 41, 64.

## CHAPTER 2

[1] Larry Crab, "When a Ministry with Singles is a Threat to the Church Leadership," *Growing Your Single Adult Ministry,* Jerry Jones, ed. (Elgin, IL: David C. Cook Publishing Co., 1994), 26.

[2] Questions for this test are based on information gleaned from *Unmarried America* by George Barna (Glendale, CA: Barna Research Group, 1993) and from the following resources as reported in various issues of *Single Adult Ministries Journal:* Questions 5 and 6, *Martial Status and Living Arrangements:* March 1992, by Arlene F. Saluter, U.S. Department of Commerce, Bureau of the Census, v.; Question 16, *American Demographics*, October 1988, 25; Question 25, *New Realities of the American Family,* by Dennis A. Ahlburg and Carol J. DeVita, (Washington, D.C.: Population Reference Bureau, Inc., August 1992), 6.

[3] Arlene F. Saluter, *Married Status and Living Arrangements: March 1992 Table 1* (U.S. Department of Commerce, Bureau of the Census), 1.

[4] George Barna, *Unmarried America* (Glendale, CA: Barna Research Group, 1993), 27-30.

[5] *U.S. Bureau of the Census, Statistical Abstract of the United States 1992* (Washington, D.C.: U.S. Government Printing Office, 1993).

[6] George Barna, *Unmarried America,* 21.

[7] Ibid., 34, citing *Family in America Survey* (Glendale, CA: Barna Research Group, 1992).

[8] Ibid., 33, citing *OmniPoll 1-91* (Glendale, CA: Barna Research Group, 1991).

[9] "People Living Alone: The Fastest Growing Household Type Since 1970," *Single Adult Ministries Journal*, January 1992, 2.

[10] "Unmarried with Children," *Ministry Currents* (Glendale, CA: Barna Research Group), April–June 1993, 14.

[11] *Child Support and Alimony: 1989* (U.S. Department of Commerce, Bureau of the Census), 1.

[12] George Barna, *Unmarried America*, 63, 64.

[13] Jim Smoke, *Center for Divorce Recovery Newsletter* (Phoenix, AZ: Center for Divorce Recovery) February-March 1990.

[14] Jim Smoke, *Growing Through Divorce* (Eugene, OR; Harvest House Publishers, 1976), 26, 27.

[15] George Barna, *Unmarried America*, 77.

[16] Sheron Patterson, "Divorce Can Result in Stigma," *The United Methodist Review* (Dallas, TX: United Methodist Communication Council), May 21, 1993, 10.

[17] Judith Wallerstein, *Second Chances: Men, Women, and Children a Decade after Divorce* (New York, NY: Ticknor & Fields, 1990), xii.

[18] *Statistical Abstract of the United States,* 1992, 446.

[19] Quoted from a stepfamily seminar offered by Dick Dunn at the National United Methodist Singles Ministry Convention, Orlando, Florida, in July 1992.

[20] *Historical Abstract of the U.S. and Historical Statistics: Colonial Times to Present* (U.S. Bureau of the Census, 1992), as quoted in *Unmarried America,* by George Barna, 87.

[21] Joseph A. Rayan, "For the Widowed: Eight Steps to Help You Begin a Ministry with This Booming Segment of the Population," *Single Adult Ministries Journal*, #99, 20. Adapted from *Loving Again* (Grand Rapids, MI: Zondervan, 1991), 188-193.

[22] George Barna, *Unmarried America*, 84.

[23] Ibid., 94.

[24] George Hunter, *How to Reach Secular People* (Nashville: Abingdon Press, 1992), 102.

[25] Donald L. Dewar, *Communication Briefings*, July 1987, 8.

[26] Terry Hershey, *Beginning Again* (Nashville, TN: Thomas Nelson Publishers, 1986), 51, 52.

## CHAPTER 3

[1] George Barna, *The Barna Report 1992-1993: An Annual Survey of Life-Styles, Values and Religious Views* (Ventura, CA: Regal Books, 1992), 72.

[2] James L. Adams, *The Care and Feeding of Ideas* (Reading, MA: Addison-Wesley Publishing Company, Inc., 1986),183.

[3] *Singles Ministry Resources National Training Seminar Notebook* (Colorado Springs, CO: Singles Ministry Resources).

[4] Reprinted with permission from *The Idea Catalog for Single Adult Ministry,* edited by Jerry Jones (Elgin, IL: David C. Cook Publishing Co., 1993), 49.

## CHAPTER 4

[1] Lyle Schaller, *Create Your Own Future!* (Nashville: Abingdon Press, 1991), 78.

[2] Ibid.

[3] George Barna, *Never on a Sunday: The Challenge of the Unchurched* (Glendale, CA: Barna Research Group, 1990), 27.

[4] Terry Hershey, as presented in a Singles Ministry Resources Leadership Training Group Seminar in Lincoln, Nebraska, on March 15, 1991.

## CHAPTER 5

[1] George Barna, *The Barna Report 1992-1993: An Annual Survey of Life-Styles, Values and Religious Views* (Ventura, CA: Regal Books, 1992), 72.

[2] "Remembering What It Feels Like to Be a Visitor," *Single Adult Ministries Journal,* October 1990, #77, 2.

[3] George Barna, *User Friendly Churches* (Ventura, CA: Regal Books, 1991), 177.

[4] John Ed Mathison, *Tried and True: Eleven Principles of Church Growth* (Nashville, TN: Discipleship Resources, 1992), 69.

[5] C. Kirk Hadaway in *Church Growth Principles,* as reported in *Net Results,* July 1993, 10.

[6] Robert Lee, *Church Planter,* January-March 1993, 1, as reported in *Current Thoughts and Trends,* April 1993, 23.

## Chapter 6

[1] George Barna, *Single Adults in America*, 28.

## Chapter 7

[1] George Barna, *User Friendly Churches, 106, 107.*

[2] Ibid., 107.

## Chapter 8

[1] George Barna, *User Friendly Churches,* 163.

[2] From *Leadership Training Group Notebook '92-'93* (Colorado Springs, CO: Singles Ministry Resources), 7.

[3] Adapted with permission from *Giving the Ministry Away* by Terry Hershey, Karen Butler, and Rich Hurst (Elgin, IL: David C. Cook Publishing Co., 1992), 80-86.

## Chapter 9

[1] Bill Flanagan, "The Financial Benefits of a Healthy Singles Ministry," *Growing Your Single Adult Ministry*, Jerry Jones, ed., 340.

[2] Herb Miller, "Shutting Off the Financial Failure Signals," *Net Results*, July 1993, 4.

## Chapter 10

[1] Rich Kraljev, "How Targeted Advertising Can Help Build Your Ministry," *Growing Your Single Adult Ministry*, Jerry Jones, ed., 352.

[2] George Barna, *Marketing the Church* (Colorado Springs: NavPress, 1988), 123.

[3] Robert Simerly, *Planning and Marketing Conferences and Workshops* (San Francisco: Jossey-Bass Publishers, 1990), 64-68.

[4] Steve Diggs, *Putting Your Best Foot Forward* (Holbrook, MASS: Bob Adams, Inc., 1990), 109, 110.

[5] Herman Holtz, *Great Promo Pieces* (New York: John Wiley and Sons, Inc., 1988), 177.

[6] John Etcheto, "Making Word-of-Mouth Advertising Work for You," *Growing Your Single Adult Ministry,* 355.

## Chapter 11

[1] From telephone interviews conducted with Anthony Pappas in May and July of 1994.

[2] Lyle Schaller, *The Seven-Day-a-Week-Church,* quoted in *Net Results,* February 1993, page 9.

[3] Steve Burt, *Activating Leadership in the Small Church* (Valley Forge, PA: Judson Press, 1988), 15.

[4] Lyle Schaller, *The Small Church Is Different!* (Nashville: Abingdon Press, 1982), 31.

[5] Richard John Neuhaus, quoted in *Current Thoughts and Trends,* December 1992, 18.

[6] Reprinted with permission from *Single Adult Ministries Journal,* March/April, 1992 (Issue #91-#92), 8. (Items 1 and 2 were adapted from an outside article by Jim Smoke in *Singles Ministry Handbook* (Wheaton, IL: Victor Books, 1989), 254-256.

## Chapter 12

[1] Herb Miller, *Net Results,* March 1991, 4.

[2] Jim Smoke, *Growing Your Single Adult Ministry,* 52.

[3] Found in *Bibliotheca Sacra,* Oct.-Dec. 1992, as summarized in *Current Thoughts and Trends,* December 1992, 21.

[4] Chris Eaton, quoted in *Singles Ministry Handbook.* edited by Doug Fagerstrom (Wheaton, IL: Victor Books, 1989), 220.

[5] Roberta Hestenes, *Turning Committees into Communities* (Colorado Springs, CO: NavPress, 1991), 5.

[6] George Barna, *Ministry Millstones: A Dozen Mistakes You Can Avoid* (Glendale, CA: Barna Research Group, 1990), 20.

[7] Richard Lovelace, *Renewal As a Way of Life* (Downers Grove, IL: InterVarsity Press, 1985), 10.

# SINGLES
## *Ministry Resources*

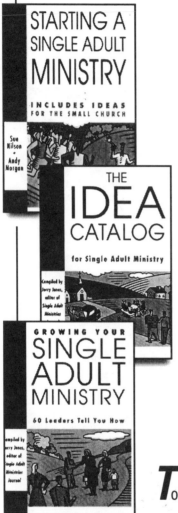
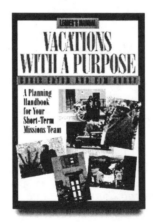

*T*o receive more information about these and other quality singles ministry resources or to order, contact your local Christian bookstore

### OR
## SINGLES MINISTRY RESOURCES
**P.O. Box 60430**
**Colorado Springs, Colorado 80960-0430**

Or call (800) 323-7543
Canada (800) 387-5856
or (719) 579-6471

*SINGLES MINISTRY RESOURCES is a division of Cook Communications Ministries*